S0-CKG-745

Japan and the United States

American University Studies

Series X
Political Science
Vol. 36

PETER LANG
New York • San Francisco • Bern • Baltimore
Frankfurt am Main • Berlin • Wien • Paris

Earl Conteh-Morgan

Japan and the United States

Global Dimensions of Economic Power

PETER LANG
New York • San Francisco • Bern • Baltimore
Frankfurt am Main • Berlin • Wien • Paris

337.52073
C76j

Library of Congress Cataloging-in-Publication Data

Conteh-Morgan, Earl.
  Japan and the United States : global dimensions of economic
power / Earl Conteh-Morgan.
      p. cm. — (American university studies. Series X, Political science ;
vol. 36)
  Includes bibliographical references.
    1. United States—Foreign economic relations—Japan.   2. Japan—
Foreign economic relations—United States.   I. Title.   II. Series :
American university studies. Series X, Political science; V. 36.
  HF1456.5.J3C655   1992   337.52073—dc20   92-13191
  ISBN 0-8204-1915-X   CIP
  ISSN 0740-0470

TP

Die Deutsche Bibliothek-CIP-Einheitsaufnahme

Conteh-Morgan, Earl:
Japan and the United States : global dimensions of economic power /
Earl Conteh-Morgan.—New York; Berlin; Bern; Frankfurt/M.; Paris;
Wien: Lang, 1992
   (American university studies : Ser. 10, Political science ; Vol. 36)
      ISBN 0-8204-1915-X
NE: American university studies/10

The paper in this book meets the guidelines for permanence and
durability of the Committee on Production Guidelines for
Book Longevity of the Council on Library Resources.

© Peter Lang Publishing, Inc., New York 1992

All rights reserved.
Reprint or reproduction, even partially, in all forms such as microfilm,
xerography, microfiche, microcard, offset strictly prohibited.

Printed in the United States of America.

To the students of North-North symmetry
who are pondering the present and contemplating the future
now that the East-West rivalry is gone
and who thereby merit our attention.

University Libraries
Carnegie Mellon University
Pittsburgh PA 15213-3890

TABLE OF CONTENTS

LIST OF TABLES AND FIGURES

ACRONYMS

ANC	African National Congress
ASEAN	Association of South-East Asian Nations
DOD	Department of Defense
EPA	Economic Planning Agency
FMS	Foreign Military Sales
FY	Fiscal Year
GATT	General Agreement on Tariffs and Trade
GSP	Generalized System of Preferences
IGOs	Inter-Governmental Organizations
IMF	International Monetary Fund
JICA	Japan International Cooperation Agency
LDCs	Less Developed Countries
MFO	Multinational Force and Observers
MITI	Ministry of International Trade and Industry
MNCs	Multinational Corporations
MOF	Ministry of Finance
MOFA	Ministry of Foreign Affairs
NASA	National Aeronautics and Space Administration
NATO	North Atlantic Treaty Organization
NICs	Newly Industrializing Countries
ODA	Official Development Assistance
OECD	Organization for Economic Cooperation and Development
OECF	Overseas Economic Cooperation Fund
OPEC	Organization of Petroleum Exporting Countries
PLO	Palestine Liberation Organization
R&D	Research and Development
SDI	Strategic Defense Initiative
SII	Structural Impediments Initiative
UN	United Nations
UNDP	United Nations Development Program
UNHCR	United Nations High Commissioner for Refugees
UNIIMOG	United Nations Iran Iraq Military Observer Group
UNRWA	United Nations Relief and Works Agency
UNTAG	United Nations Transition Group
USFJ	United States Forces, Japan

PREFACE

Change, adaptation, conflict and cooperation have been major elements of the startling transformation of the international political and economic landscape in the past few years, culminating in an ongoing redefinition and reconceptualization of security. In the political, economic, and military arenas, rapid changes in East-West, and United States-Japan relations are dramatically transforming the structure of postwar international politics, placing far greater importance on the role of the economy and technology as elements of national strength. Accordingly, the European Community, the United States-Canada-Mexico Free Trade arrangements, Japan and the Pacific Rim, and other potential and real economic schemes are attracting a great deal of debate, reports, and scholarly analysis. Japan's phenomenal economic success has become almost an obsession in the United States especially when viewed in terms of the perennial discussion of a United States in relative economic and/or hegemonic decline. This book's overall objective is to offer a comprehensive and theoretical analysis of change and adaptation, conflict and cooperation in United States-Japan relations in the context of their power economic capabilities. A second objective is to provide an informed, balanced, and critical understanding of Japan's ongoing globalist orientation in the context of the turbulence in the international system. It is also an attempt to reconceptualize and redefine the structure of the evolving global system based in part on the notion of hegemonic stability, which I hope will open new avenues of analysis and research. This book is therefore intended for all those who must describe, explain, or engage in prediction and prescription about Japan's globalist orientation, or United States-Japan power economic interactions in the wider context of international systemic changes. The reader will find a substantial dosage of Japanese and American foreign policies, international political economy, and Third World politics as they relate to the United States-Japan global dimensions of economic power.

I am deeply grateful to the University of South Florida's Research Council for awarding me International Travel Grants which made it possible to travel to conferences to exchange ideas with other scholars on the major themes discussed in this book. Needless to say, without the Council's support this project would have been almost impossible to complete. My profound thanks are also due to the following individuals: Marianne Bell, Carole Rennick, and Toshua King of the Information Processing Center at the University of South Florida. In particular, Dr. Mark Orr of the Center for International Affairs, Dr. Alvin Wolfe of the Department of Anthropology, Dr. Festus Ohaegbulam, and Dr. Susan MacManus both of the Department of Government and International Affairs, have all in one way or the other, influenced the completion of this book. Finally, I would also like to thank Donna Britton, Cynthia Craig, Nanette Barkey, Joan Newcomb, and John Bradley for their individual contributions and moral support.

Earl Conteh-Morgan

College of Arts and Sciences
University of South Florida
Tampa, Florida 1992

1

INTRODUCTION

"The old order changeth, yielding placc to ncw," wrotc thc English Poet Laureate, Alfred Lord Tennyson.[1] Although written in the nineteenth century this verse is particularly *a propos* to the dramatic changes witnessed by the world especially in the last three years. The already startling transformation of the international landscape has generated a mushrooming of works trying to capture the dizzying pace of change and its accompanying uncertainty. Among the many scholarly works focusing on these winds of change are: *Turbulence in World Politics* by James Rosenau, *The Rise and Fall of the Great Powers* by Paul Kennedy; *After Hegemony: Cooperation and Discord in the World Political System* by Robert Keohane, and *The New Democracies* by Brad Roberts, among others.[2] The reality is that no sooner such works on the international system are out than they become largely outdated. The popular movements for democracy in Eastern and Central Europe, the clamor for multiparty systems in many African countries, the increasing consolidation of regional trading blocs in Europe and the Americas, Japan's rapid economic rise in the international community, and the virtual end of the Cold War rivalry, among others, constitute some of the elements of global change whose repercussions signal the imminent collapse of the post-World War II international political economy and United States hegemonic leadership.

The repeated reference to a "New World Order" implies that some of the most fundamental political and economic assumptions on which this international system has operated are being rapidly undermined. The world interdependence in practice competes with regionalism as evidenced by the trend toward the formation of regional blocs—the European Community and the U.S.-Canada-Mexico Free Trade agreements are cases in point. The profound changes have engaged the global consciousness to such an extent that references are already being made to

new global roles for the United States and Japan in a multipolar world with
speculations that the balance of economic and military power in the next twenty-
five to fifty years will be fundamentally altered to produce either a "Bigemony,"
a Pax Consortis, a Pax Americana Phase II, or a Pax Nipponica.[3]

The reference to these four scenarios for the future are a manifestation
undoubtedly of the view that has largely gained currency of United States relative
hegemonic decline. Such decline is manifested in the United States domestic
economy where the family accounts are largely kept in the red each month. In fact
since 1986, America's household budgets have registered an aggregate deficit.
The opposite is the case with Japan where households on average save three times
more of their annual income compared to what American households save. In
1989, it was 17 percent to 19 percent for Japanese households and less than 5
percent for American households.[4]

The changing roles of Japan and the United States in the international system
are especially at the core of change in the global economy because of their
centrality to a stable world economy and to a peaceful international system. The
relative hegemonic decline of the United States and changes in the international
industrial structure have shifted the relative economic power of the advanced
industrial nations and therefore focused managerial and academic attention in
theorizing about a new international economic order. The Japanese themselves
have come to the realization that the changing global and economic political
landscape requires them to exercise more adaptive skills in foreign policy if they
are to enhance their economic security.

In December 1981, the Industrial Structure Council of Japan, an arm of the
Ministry of International Trade and Industry (MITI), appointed a subcommittee of
experts to study the question of economic security. The report of the subcommittee released in April 1982 stressed the importance of a comprehensive approach
to enhancing economic security. It recommended *inter alia* the following: (1) the
importance of conventional economic and technical aids to developing countries
as well as cultural and educational exchange programs of economic security; (2)
the need for Japan to work hard toward a greater harmonization of North-South
as well as East-West relations as a way of safeguarding its long term economic
security; (3) an increase in world food production as the best way to ensure
Japan's food security which means an expansion of aid in agricultural technology,
export credit for fertilizers, and other means of raising agricultural productivity of

the less developed food-producing countries; and (4) a need for Japan to work towards peace in geostrategic regions like the Suez and Panama Canals, Cape of Good Hope, Straits of Hormuz and the like, which are salient to Japan's economic security in terms of stability of maritime transportation.[5] These recommendations in addition to those not listed above, underscore a holistic approach to enhancing Japan's economic security with military security implications as well.

R. Taggant Murphy, writing in the *Harvard Business Review* in 1989, stated that all the leading Wall Street companies have less capital than Nomura Securities, one of the Big Four securities houses in Japan. The Japanese Postal Savings System in 1989 had assets of nearly a trillion dollars, surpassing the top twelve United States banks combined.[6] The significance of Japan's power economic capabilities is equally enormous with profound implications for global economic stability. It is generally believed that the stock market crash of October 1987 was started in Tokyo by Japanese institutional investors, and Japanese regulators then stopped it by employing the economic capabilities of the Big Four (Nomura, Daiwa, Nikko, and Yamaichi) securities houses, to prop up the market. As an event, the stock market crash is a reflection of the impact of Japan's concentrated wealth. It is also a strong indication that Japan has replaced the United States as the world financial leader. Profound changes like this and others mean that the new and evolving items on the global agenda of the international political economy need to be examined in relation to Japan's power economic capabilities, its adaptive behavior in response to global changes, and its relationship with the United States.

This study is about Japan's economic power projection in the regions of Asia, the Middle East, Africa, and Latin America. It is also about Japan's economic power and its interface with United States relative hegemonic decline. Is Japan transforming its economic power into political power in order to fulfill the global responsibilities that go with financial power? What are the indicators of Japan's globalist behavior? Are the Japanese beginning to think like the British in the nineteenth century and the United States after World War II in terms of a sense of mission to spread a political ideology and promote economic growth and stability? These are only a few of the questions that this study explores.

The next section provides a theoretical framework for analysis, a broad overview of the attributes of the system within which Japan operates and within which United States-Japan interaction takes place. It also includes further reference to the items on the global agenda, a definition of concepts, and an exposition of the theoretical argument of the entire study. Chapter two examines elements of Japan's economic expansionism—aid, trade and investment—as an integral aspect of its globalist behavior. The goals of comprehensive security, internationalization, economic security, among others are analyzed in relation to regional politics, strategic countries, and crisis situations in developing countries. What are the characteristics of Japan's economic expansionist behavior? How do political and economic factors interface to affect Japan's globalism? These are some of the questions examined in relation to Japan's economic power projection. As Japan increasingly faces the challenges of its new status as an economic superpower, its foreign aid program has become the subject of extensive analysis, reports, and debates in relation to the relative hegemonic decline of the United States, the apparent 'aid fatigue' of Western donors, the ever present demands of developing countries, and the changing political and economic landscape of the former Communist bloc and Western Europe. Chapter three underscores Japan's foreign aid articulation into its push for globalism. It identifies the various power economic roles resource transfer plays in a world system characterized by dramatic political, economic, and military changes.

The dizzying pace of change in the international political economy is mirrored in the evolving character of technological interdependence among the advanced industrial nations spawning a steadily growing level of competition among them. The United States, in particular, is having to confront the fact that the unfolding trend of technological parity with Japan and other industrialized nations has virtually eroded the preeminent position it once occupied in science and technology. The consequence is a growing loss of confidence increasingly manifested in the form of selective protectionism. Chapter four examines this technological relationship between the United States and Japan by focusing on the evolving character of technological exchange, friction, research, and convergence between the two nations. In the process, the issues of United States global competitiveness, Japan's technological contributions to United States security, and areas of policy agreements and disagreements are underscored as aspects of internal and external imperatives affecting both countries. While the focus is on broad international issues of interest to the United States and Japan, the discussion at the same time does not ignore the intensive examination of the domestic-external imperatives affecting the science and technology policies of the two nations.

The eruption of volatile and explosive situations in the Middle East since the 1980s has generated a noticeable security cooperation among Western powers and Japan. This was manifested in the multinational naval presence in the Gulf region, the extension of security assistance, the collective minesweeping operation in the Red Sea in the Summer of 1984, and the more recent multinational force assembled against Iraq in 1991. In the last decade there have been repeated calls for collective responses to crises that affect Europe and Japan more than the United States. Accordingly, the United States-Japan relationship has also been underpinned by the perennial United States demand for Japan to contribute more to global stability and increase its defense spending—that is increase its defense and overall security burden sharing. Chapter five examines the military technological cooperation between the two nations, explores the issue of burden sharing and its implications with regard to Japan's domestic political imperatives, and analyzes the interface of Japan's global security objectives and America's global security commitments in Third World regions.

Chapter six explores the gradual transformation in United States-Japan relationship as a consequence of relative United States hegemonic decline. It argues that this trend has produced a new "regime" to manage United States-Japan bilateral trade relations. This new regime is manifested in a shift from the "positive cooperation" at the height of United States hegemonic leadership to the "adversarial cooperation" generated by United States' relative economic decline and reinforced by United States-Japan culture incompatibilities. The consequence of the shift in cooperative relationship is a trend toward managed hegemony or global partnership as manifested in the recent Persian Gulf crisis in which the United States exercised overwhelming military dominance ("sticks"), while at the same time putting pressure on Japan and other allies to provide the financial support ("carrots").

The first three chapters focus on specific factors that constitute Japan's globalist orientation in the context of a changing environment. The next three chapters discuss particular issues in the United States-Japan relationship with an emphasis on their impact on conflict, cooperation, or mutual power-dependence in a turbulent global order. While this book focuses on the United States-Japan relationship and its relevance to global order, we do not wish to suggest that the existence of other major powers and their interactions with the United States is not relevant to systemic stability. Accordingly, the concluding chapter transcends the narrow focus on the United States-Japan relationship to emphasize a holistic view of a new and evolving global order, and to offer an alternative interpretation of both the changing United States-Japan relationship and the evolving structure of a new global order.   The purpose of this book is to provide a conceptual framework within which to fully appreciate the changing agenda of issues in an increasingly multipolar international system where the United States and Japan, among other actors, are constantly reminded of the need to reexamine their traditional roles.

Theoretical Framework: Power Economics and Global Change

The latter part of the 1980s was characterized by a complex mix of both startling changes and a continuous reevaluation of roles, responsibilities and obligations by the advanced industrial countries. The changes have generated concerns about the continuing stability of the contemporary global economic and military security order; in particular, about the adequacy of current "rules" governing economic and military-security relations between Japan and the United States. In other words, in the international system, the distribution of international power makes regimes possible.   However, as we have already stated, this distribution itself is undergoing tremendous upheaval related in part to the uncertainty and instability that challenge many of the political and economic accommodations that have served as the stable foundation of both the United States-Japan relationship in particular, and the international political economy in general.

Krasner and Gilpin borrowing from Kindelberger's hegemonic-stability thesis have studied the notion of regime stability extensively. His study of the depression years of the 1930s had led Kindelberger to conclude that regimes required the leadership of a hegemonic power for stability. He further argued that free trade, comparative advantage, and other elements of classical economics were by themselves inadequate and therefore required the leadership of a large and dominant economy with a natural propensity for open trade.[7] The continuous polarization of power, some would argue, that is currently taking place, would result in global economic instability and fragmentation of regimes. Thus much of the relative stability of the post-World War II international economic order has been attributed to the presence of the United States with its strong and large economy, and its effective control and domination.

Cowhey views international regimes as having two main interrelated dimension: a "commerce system" comprised of principles, rules, and decision-making processes governing the movement of international trade and investment capital; and principles and rules coordinating the management of macroeconomic policy involving to a certain extent the conduct of monetary policy to facilitate international commerce.[8] In other words, regimes represent international collective goods because they are problem solvers perceived to be beneficial to all nations. At the same time, the effectiveness of international regimes, considering the anarchic world depends primarily on the concentration of political and economic power in a relatively small number of countries. In particular, the hegemon has effective capabilities to punish or threaten, enormous resources to offer inducements and incentives, as instruments to maintain the stability of this international collective goods process. The interaction and mutually-reinforcing effect of these two types of power political and power economic instruments give the hegemon substantial power over the setting of the international agenda and the character of international cooperation.

The various theorists of hegemonic stability all underscore the two dimensions of a hegemon's power: power economic and power politico-military capabilities. Keohane identified four factors, control over which the hegemon's economic power depended: raw materials, sources of capital, markets, and "comparative advantages in the production of highly valued goods."[9] In Marxian logic it could be argued that the power economic capabilities served as a base in stabilizing the global economic order, whereas the politico-military power served as a superstructure holding intact the various interacting elements of the system and protecting them mostly from powerful and hostile extra-systemic actors. According to Keohane, "sufficient military power to protect an international political economy from incursions by hostile powers is indeed a necessary condition for successful hegemony."[10] When, however, we introduce the diverging views of realism and complex interdependence in international relations theory, then the utility of force itself is seen in a different perspective. Only once in a while is direct military power of great utility in dealing with other regime members. Most of the time it is of limited utility because few would argue that the United States would use its military advantage to press for economic concessions from the other regime members.

Direct military force and regime stability fall squarely within the realist school of thought with its emphasis on behavior in terms of power configurations within the international system.   On the other hand, the international political economy is conceptualized as anchored on interdependence, an approach that puts less emphasis on hegemonic leadership, and points to the declining utility of force in the post World War II period.   Proponents of this approach, in particular Keohane, emphasize instead a pattern of bargaining and negotiations, and of interest-based agenda-setting.   While not rejecting the notion of hegemonic leadership, Keohane maintains that liberal economic regimes could be maintained on the basis of "shared interest" of the regime members.[11]   Hegemonic stability thesis has many critics.   Some even argue that a liberal international economic order could function without a hegemon.   System-wide cooperation is considered by others to be just as effective as a hegemonic leadership.   Still others make reference to a system supporter as a way of modifying the thesis.   Chapter six of this study which specifically examines the thesis in relation to the United States-Japan relationship delves into further aspects of the thesis including some of its weaknesses.

From Hegemonic Dependence to Mutual Power-Dependence

In this section, we now begin to outline the key features of our theoretical model, and finally argue in favor of reconceptualizing the United States-Japan relationship based on the profound changes impacting on the power economic and power political capabilities of the two nations.   Implicit in this theoretical model is the notion of a shift in economic power from the overwhelming monopoly of the United States to a mutual power-dependence relationship between the United States and Japan.   Japan by virtue of its international economic position has begun to impact in a profound way the global economic order—one vivid evidence being the stock market crash of October 1987.   This development is, of course, related to a gradual erosion of United States hegemony especially as Japan continues to contribute to international regime stability by abandoning its early mercantilism policies and assuming greater global responsibilities either unilaterally or in collaboration with the United States.   In short, we argue that the whole trend is manifested in Japan's increasing globalist behavior.

The startling developments in the international economic order are very significant when put in the context of Lake's reference to the weakness of a non-hegemonic regime. Such a regime would be unstable because of the strong proclivity to protectionism and to cheating generated by the high levels of uncertainty in the operating environment. The consequence is a fragile regime characterized by broken promises and a strong incentive to cheat.[12] Ordinarily, a decline in international hegemony may destabilize the economic order which in turn may increase the level of transaction costs—costs of information, bargaining, enforcement of contracts, and the like. In short, it increases the risk that a country will renege on its commitments in international economic arrangements, and raises the possibility of a more pronounced clash between differences in macroeconomic and microeconomic policies among the major economic powers.

In essence we argue that the shift from Japan's dependence on the United States to increasing mutual power-dependence also requires more global involvement by Japan and increased burden sharing, all a reflection of a process of gradual reorganization in the United States-Japan relationship in particular, and in the international regime in general. The components of Figure 1.1 and the arrows connecting them represent the (assumed) structure of Japan's involvement in the global system. It is selective and closed because no other determinants of globalism than power economics and no other determinants of power economics than globalism and their effects are identified for particular examination. It is assumed that the influence of power economics on globalism can be analyzed without the introduction of intervening factors. The key influence of power economic factors on Japanese globalism are, in turn, supposed to occur not directly but through the efforts undertaken to pursue global objectives and responsibilities, the specifics of Japanese dependence on the United States, and the United States-Japanese relationship of mutual power-dependence. All of these second-order elements are also assumed to influence Japan's global behavior and each other.

The conceptual clarifications of the model are as follows:

Power Economics refers to the whole range of economic instruments and techniques employed in the pursuit of global objectives and in the case of Japan, at times to satisfy international expectations. It is both a means and an end to globalism.[13] Japan's foreign assistance represents a central component of its power economic behavior because it articulates specifically into the process of globalism in the form of loans, grants, technical assistance, Japanese Volunteers abroad, investments, and the like. Economic power often implies political power and vice versa because of the inherent overlap between politics and economics.

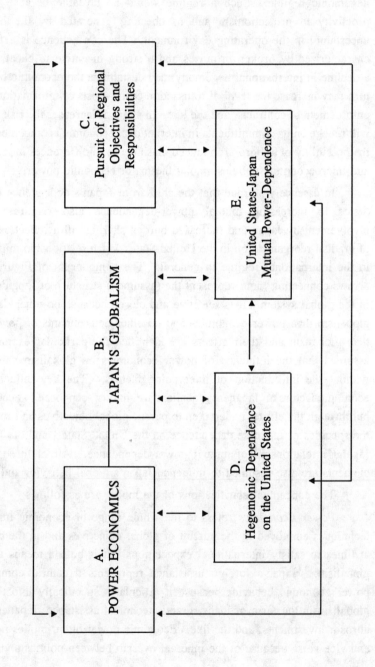

Figure 1.1 Power Economics and Globalism: A Model for Analysis
of the United States-Japan Relationship

In the case of Japan its economic power reflected in its power economic behavior is steadily enhancing its overall power capabilities such that it is rapidly being thrust into more international political roles and entanglements like peace keeping, the Arab-Israeli conflict, the South African Apartheid issue, Persian Gulf security, and increasing military burden sharing with the United States. In other words, a primarily economic oriented nation is rapidly being propelled into a politically oriented nation.

The term *globalism* refers to an outlook that is worldwide in scope and structured by internationalized power economic and power political behavior. It refers to Japan's involvement in debt, aid, trade and investment, and military security issues around the world. It is, in short, the sum total of the actual or potential growing involvement in international politico-military and socio-economic issues.

Pursuit of regional objectives and responsibilities means the efforts by Japan to promote and safeguard its economic interests around the world, in particular, in developing regions; to help alleviate problems in developing countries related to debt, agriculture, population, and development in general, that both in the short term and the long term will be beneficial to Japan itself and the rest of the international system.

By *hegemonic dependence on the United States* we refer to the immediate post-World War II period, and situations in the present period in which the political and economic policies of Japan were and/or are conditioned, by the overall policies of the United States to which Japan is subjected.[14] In particular, it refers to the whole spectrum of United States international economic, political and military leadership on which Japan relied to operate in the global environment and pursue its own objectives. In many instances, Japan's power economic and power political behavior is largely a reflection of United States power economic and power political behavior, which can have either a constraining or stimulating effect on Japan's globalism. In the United States-Japan relationship dependence is a structural condition in which Japan is dependent on the United States for say nuclear protection and other forms of military-security concerns, without which Japan would be sensitive or vulnerable to external threats from say the former Soviet Union or China, of the cut-off of Middle Eastern oil because of instability in the Persian Gulf.

Finally, *mutual power-dependence* refers to the whole range of United States-Japan transactions structured by symmetrical power relations in the process of bargaining or negotiations. Drawing largely upon the author's previous analysis of mutual power-dependence, the United States-Japan relationship is structured by four factors.[15] First, neither nation is in a dominant politico-economic position because neither can terminate the relationship without great loss or cost to its global security. Second, the mutual possession of valued things ('utilities') by both countries places them in advantageous bargaining positions, which may enable them to dictate a number of conditions to each other on the basis of which concessions are made. Third, the types of transactions involved allow both countries to intervene and exercise leverage in each other's internal and external affairs. Fourth, joint cooperative activities in aid, trade and investment, and military security require that both countries bargain and negotiate on symmetrical terms which again place both of them in advantageous bargaining positions.

In this study the role of power economics is purposively underscored without outrightly ignoring the possibility of other immediate causes of Japan's globalism. One central question is to *what extent* is Japanese globalism dependent on Japanese power economics and how are they in turn related to evolving Japanese international power politics in general? The emphasis is, in other words, placed on how globalism results from power economics and from the dynamic interaction of power economics and globalist orientations. This in particular enables us to identify types of recurrent dynamic links between power economics and globalism.

The next set of questions that come readily to mind have to do with the pursuit of global objectives and responsibilities. What is the scope and intensity of Japanese political and economic activities in the Third World? What are the underlying rationales for pursuit of these objectives and assumption of these responsibilities? How effectively are power economic capabilities (especially foreign aid) used in the pursuit of goals and the meeting of commitments? The arrow connecting power economics and the pursuit of global objectives and responsibilities directly with each other suggests its own questions: what roles do power economic capabilities play in Third World regions? To what extent and how does Japan marshal and distribute its power economic capabilities to achieve its objectives and meet its regional commitments to recipient countries?

To gain a better understanding of the dynamics of Japan's globalism, it is also worthwhile to examine how globalism may influence the use of power economic capabilities which have given rise to it. It is necessary to ask: in what kind of power economic and globalist objective is Japan likely to adopt active economic, political, and military roles? The reasoning here is that no doubt the globalism of Japan is bound to have an impact on power economic factors in cases where crisis situations develop, or where obstacles, threats, or competition are encountered in the international system. In this respect the Arab-Israeli conflict, the Persian Gulf, or South Africa quickly come to mind, as well as regional conflicts with serious implications for the promotion of Japanese regional economic objectives.

Besides, the elements of globalism may affect not only the pursuit of global objectives and responsibilities, but also influence directly the globalist behavior and the tactics of achieving goals and fulfilling responsibilities undertaken. For example, the use of foreign economic aid as a substitute for military aid in zones of conflict may essentially affect the rationales underlying the economic oriented globalism of Japan.

Furthermore, the pursuit of global objectives and responsibilities may be both enhanced and constrained by Japan's dependence on the United States in some areas of international relations. For example, the traditional Japanese dependence on the United States for military protection has made Japan a largely economic-oriented nation politically reluctant to, and constrained by Article 9 of its constitution to engage in militarism or in substantial defense spending.[16] Also, the traditional reliance on United States hegemonic power has led many observers to conclude that Japan lacks the willingness and experience to play the role of a hegemonic power that Great Britain played in the nineteenth century and the United States since the end of World War II. On the other hand, it is argued by many that Japan's defense "free ride" on the United States, releases the money it could have used for defense to promote its global interests. To gain a better understanding of the overall structure and dynamics of Japan's globalist orientation, this set of questions needs to be examined in more detail and in relation to hegemonic stability.

The increasing mutual power dependence relationship between the United States and Japan affects Japan's global orientation and the pursuit of its objectives and responsibilities. On the one hand, the more military, technological, and economic cooperation the two states engage in at a level of symmetry, the more political power and global influence Japan accumulates in the process. On the other hand, the less cooperation that results in the mutual power-dependence process, the more likely it is that Japan will complement United States efforts in regional issues like development, debt, or military security; and the less likely is Japan to learn and effectively perform the role of a global hegemonic power.

It is worth noting that all of the components of the model and their connections with one another may be viewed as a simultaneous and continuous interactive process contributing to the globalism of Japan. The subsequent chapters will identify and underscore the various factors, events, and issues to present a dynamic and general picture of Japan's globalist orientation.

In short, we argue that Japan's increasing globalism due to its power economic capabilities is steadily transforming the United States-Japan relationship and thereby helping to shape the character of United States hegemonic leadership in an era of many dramatic changes in the international system. We will, accordingly, explore the role of power economics in the transformation of a primarily economic power into a more globalist power increasingly being confronted by political and military issues, and steadily losing its dependence on its hegemon ally.

We have already made a number of references to United States hegemonic decline. This means that this study is largely predicated on the argument that the U.S. has experienced relative   hegemonic decline vis-a-vis other advanced industrial nations. Before it entered World War II in 1941, it produced about a third of the world's manufactures, but by the end of the war in 1945 its share of world manufacturing output was approximately half—the first time ever that a single nation has ever attained such economic power. Western Europe was ravaged by the war and literally lay in ruins, whilst Japan was a defeated and occupied country. Soviet transportation, agriculture, and infrastructure in general was no match for U.S. economic power. In other words, the U.S. possessed overwhelming power economic capabilities in relation to any other nation. It produced over 50 percent of the world's steel, 49 percent of its energy, possessed gold reserves of $20 billion, close to two-thirds of the world's total of $33 billion, and its GNP was about nearly half of the world's total.[17] In the military sphere, the U.S. had monopoly over the nuclear weapon; the only threat was that the former Soviet Union had 28 percent of the world's troops in contrast to 9 percent for the United States.[18] The U.S. even up to the early 1970s was so overwhelmingly superior in economic and military capabilities that a greater part of the Third

World was willing and encouraged to emulate American versions of capitalism and democracy.

The preponderant economic and political power capabilities naturally translated into numerous global commitments and a leadership position. This new role was manifested in interventions in Greece and Turkey to contain Soviet Communism, leadership positions in a network of regional defense organizations, and ensuring safety and access through sea lanes of trade. By the early 1970s, there were already references being made to a U.S. overcommitted with a network of over 300 overseas military bases, over 1 million soldiers in 30 countries, and mutual defense treaties with 42 nations.

Beginning with the 1960s, the U.S. seemed to have started encountering economic difficulties. It was rapidly losing its preponderant economic and military position of 1945. It was experiencing a loss in the relative share of the world's GNP, production, trade, and technological leadership. By 1980 according to CIA statistics the American share of world GNP dropped from 25.9 percent in 1960 to 21.5 percent in 1980.[19]

The domestic and foreign policies of both Presidents Kennedy and Johnson were significant in setting the stage for a troubled U.S. economy in the future. Both presidents increased American military expenditure overseas in large part because of Vietnam and the need to contain communism in other parts of the Third World. In their domestic policies they favored increases in domestic expenditures but resisted the political costs of raising taxes to pay for the inflationary outcomes. The consequence was a gradual weakening of the economy manifested in increasing government deficits, rapid price increases, and growing U.S. industrial uncompetitiveness. By the mid 1970s, the U.S. share of world gold reserves (excluding the Communist bloc) decreased substantially from 68 percent in 1950 to only 27 percent in 1973.[20] The combined effect of growing balance of payments deficits, a decrease in gold reserves, and continued overseas commitments and domestic expenditures forced the Nixon Administration to end the dollar's link to gold in private markets, and then to float the dollar against other currencies. The Bretton Woods System, an integral part of American global leadership collapsed with a steady decrease in U.S. economic preeminence.

In absolute terms, the U.S. is currently much richer than in the first decade after World War II. Its citizens are also much better off in absolute terms. The gradual relative economic decline is manifested primarily in the instability of its finances.   Its staggering trade deficit which since the mid 1980s has easily surpassed the $150 billion mark every year is a combination of the uncompetitiveness of U.S. industrial products in foreign markets, and declining sales of agricultural exports.   The industrial decline has also been manifested in both older manufactures—textiles, iron, steel, shipbuilding, and the like—and in basic manufactures—robotics, aerospace technology, automobiles, machine tools, and computers.   In agriculture the success of the Green Revolution in many Third World countries has undermined American food export competitiveness. Moreover, the European Community (EC) because of its Common Agricultural Policy (CAP) which heavily subsidizes European farmers, has become a major producer of agricultural surpluses.[21]   This seeming abundance of food availability in the world has contributed to drastic declines in agricultural prices and in American food exports, and thus contributed to the bankruptcy of many American farmers.

The staggering decline in U.S. earning power manifested in a huge national debt has led the U.S. to import increasingly larger amounts of capital to handle its expenses around the world.   This trend had by the mid 1980s transformed the nation from the world's largest creditor to the world's largest debtor nation.   For the obvious reasons outlined above the U.S. has been urging and pressuring its rich allies, Japan in particular, to engage in burden sharing, and adopt more fair trade practices.   The changing U.S. leadership position is thus manifested in conflict and cooperation, change and adaptation in its relationship with Japan and the EC.   President Bush's January 1992 trip to Japan is an example of the dilemma of a once preponderant U.S. in relative decline.   United States-Japan economic disputes and talks relating to automobiles, computers, and other items are now a perennial issue.

Endnotes

1 Alfred Lord Tennyson, *The Passing of Arthur*.

2 James N. Rosenau, *Turbulence in World Politics: A Theory of Change and Continuity*, (Princeton: Princeton University Press, 1991); Paul Kennedy, *The Rise and Fall of the Great Powers* (New York: Random House, 1987); Robert O. Keohane, *After Hegemony: Cooperation and Discord in the World Political Economy* (Princeton: Princeton University Press, 1984); and Brad Roberts (ed.), *The New Democracies: Global Change and U.S. Policy* (Cambridge: MIT Press, 1991).

3 For further details on these future scenarios, see, Takashi Inoguchi, "Japan's Global Role in a Multipolar World," in Shafigul Islam (ed.) *Yen For Development: Japanese Foreign Aid and the Politics of Burden Sharing* (New York: Council on Foreign Relations Press, 1991), pp. 11–26.

4 See, for example, Kazuhiko Nagato, "The Japan-U.S. Savings-Rate Gap," *Economic Eye*, June 1985, pp 228–235.

5 Ministry of International Trade and Industry (MITI), *Economic Security in Japan*, Tokyo, 1982.

6 R. Taggart Murphy, "Power Without Purpose: The Crisis of Japan's Financial Dominance," *Harvard Business Review*, March-April 1989, p. 72.

7 C.P. Kindelberger, *The World in Depression, 1929–1939* (Harmondsworth: Allen Lane, The Penguin Press, 1973).

8 Peter F. Cowhey, "The Agenda of the Leading Nations for the World Economy: A Theory of International Economic Regimes," in Gunter Heiduk and Kozo Yamamura (eds.) *Technological Competition and Interdependence: The Search for Policy in the United States, West Germany, and Japan* (Seattle: University of Washington Press, 1990) pp. 107–150.

9 Robert O. Keohane, *After Hegemony: Cooperation and Discord in the World Political Economy* (Princeton: Princeton University Press, 1984) p. 32.

10 Robert O. Keohane, *After Hegemony: Cooperation and Discord in the World Political Economy*, p. 136.

11 Robert O. Keohane, *After Hegemony: Cooperation and Discord in the World Political Economy*, especially chapter 4, pp. 50–51.

12 D.A. Lake, "Beneath the Commerce of Nations: A Theory of International Economic Structures," *International Studies Quarterly* 1984, 28:143.

13 Details on the application of economic instruments of policy can be found in Charles P. Kinderlberger, *Power and money: The Economics of International Politics and the Politics of International Economics* (New York: Basic Books, 1970); David A. Baldwin, *Economic Statecraft* (Princeton: Princeton University Press, 1985); and Joan M. Nelson, *Aid, Influence and Foreign Policy* (New York: Macmillan, 1968).

14 Conceptual clarifications of dependence and dependency are found in James A. Caporaso, "Dependence, Dependency, and Power in the Global System: A Structural and Behavioral Analysis," *International Organization* 32, No. 1 (Winter 1978).

15 See, for example, S.B. Bachrach, and E.J. Lawler, "The Perception of Power," *Social Forces* 55 (1976): 123–134; O.R. Young (ed.) *Bargaining: Formal Theories of Negotiation* (Chicago: University of Illinois Press, 1975); and E. Conteh-Morgan, *American Foreign Aid and Global Power Projection*, (Aldershot: Dartmouth Publishing Company, 1990), ch. 9.

16 For further details on the constraining effects of the Japanese constitution on its foreign policy, see Reinhard Drifte, *Japan's Foreign Policy* (New York: Council on Foreign Relations Press, 1990) Chapters 1–4.

17 See, for example, B.M. Rowland (ed.) *Balance of Power or Hegemony: The Inter-War Monetary System* (New York: Alfred A. Knopf, 1976) p. 220

18 For further details, see, Paul Kennedy *The Rise and Fall of the Great Powers* (New York: Random House, 1987) Chapter 7.

19 *CIA, Handbook of Economic Statistics*, 1984, p. 4.

20 For further details, see W.H. Becker, and S.F. Wells, Jr. (eds.) *Economics and World Power: An Assessment of American Diplomacy Since 1789* (New York, Columbia University Press 1984); and J. Gowa, *Closing the Gold Window: Domestic Politics and the End of Bretton Woods* (Ithaca, New York: Cornell University Press, 1983).

21 See, for example, Paul Kennedy, *The Rise and Fall of the Great Powers*, pp. 525–526.

2

ECONOMIC INTERDEPENDENCE AND
REGIONAL POWER POLITICS

It sounds crudely simplistic, but economic power usually interfaces with political issues in foreign markets, and political expediency is usually needed to maintain and protect economic relationships. If, however, the geographic boundaries of the market become too volatile, explosive, and dangerous to maintain relationships with, then that is likely to lead to a retrenchment by the foreign power within that region, or a reluctance to expand economic relationships. In the same way, if the region is endowed with strategic resources necessary for the economic viability of the foreign power, then that is likely to create a dilemma for the foreign power that could lead to intervention, political involvement, or a costly redirection of economic relationships. For example, the interaction of advanced industrial powers with the Middle East and its critical oil deposits shows a very significant correlation between regional stability and Western defense of uninterrupted access to oil.

An important consequence of a globalist economic behavior is the fact that economic interdependence establishes a power-political relationship among interacting states. In theory, economic activities are sometimes assumed to be largely insulated from purely political issues. In practice, however, economic advantages are transformed into political instruments to gain short-term or long-term economic and/or political objectives. In international politics economic interdependence creates vulnerabilities that can be exploited and manipulated to achieve objectives. In combination with other objectives, regional actors attempt to achieve their own political objectives by transforming dependence and power relations into a political weapon. Predominantly economic oriented states, like Japan, seek to protect themselves from the existing regional political disputes in many Third World regions. The balancing act to pursue economic objectives and at the same time avoid being entangled in regional conflicts has become a major feature of international relations in the contemporary global system.

In the Third World, with many different geographic and cultural divisions, economic activities and political situations give rise to different outcomes when they are intertwined with local issues. Economic activities are affected by political and social issues and similarly political realities are affected by the economic behavior of major powers. The Third World, in particular, is a universe of numerous conflict situations and seemingly intractable disputes in which the pursuit of regional objectives is determined as much by a region's strategic importance as it is by the existing regional conflict. The prevalence of a fundamental harmony of interests is most often invalid, and the pursuit of regional economic objectives in a politically volatile region has profound effects on globalism as a basis of foreign policy.

The central thrust of this chapter, then, is the intersection of regional economic objectives and political realities in Japan's globalist behavior in the Third World. Integral to this relationship of economics and politics are three closely related issues of importance to international political economy. The first is the way in which economic interdependence affects and is affected by hot regional issues. Second, is the adaptive behavior of a major economic power, in this case Japan, to the vicissitudes of regional politics. The third is the effect of global changes (especially the superpower neo-detente and U.S. economic hegemonic decline) on Japan's global concerns with aid, trade, investment, and debt relief in the Third World.

For Japan the definition of national borders is rapidly changing as its global economic activities expand. The steady growth of aid, trade, investments, and involvement in regional problem solutions are resulting in an internationalization of corporate activity and a deepening of interdependence.[1] In particular, the rapid increase in Japanese direct foreign investment and foreign trade expansion since the recent appreciation of the yen has resulted in dynamic development of global management structures which transcend national borders. What has been referred to as the new globalism of Japan is manifested in a three-pronged economic cooperation strategy of assistance, trade and investment, and in provision of 'technology'. Additionally, it is also manifested in attitudinal transformation into an increasingly internationalist mindset characterized by: greater use of economic and technical and other forms of power, establishing international solidarity through international contributions, cooperative activities, interdependence and other means.

This new globalism on the part of Japan is a consequence of the profound changes experienced in the international economy during the 1970s. The consequent push for "comprehensive security" is widely recognized and based on the strong awareness of the interlocking relationship between Japan's economy and peace and stability of the world. This finds expression in initiatives such as the Pacific Basin Cooperation Concept, debt relief proposals for Third World countries, or the increase in real terms of ODA in the midst of severe budgetary restrictions.

Expansionism and Imperatives in Asia

In various regions of the world Japan's economic power spawns various reactions. In Asia its economic success has made it a source of some amount of regional pride. It is also the most important source of development resources in the region. In still other regions of Asia, memories of Japanese military aggression and atrocities during World War II still affect relations with the Japanese. However, in the overall process of global economic power projection—aid, trade and investment pursuits—Japan possesses assets that most other advanced industrial countries lack. Japan has no legacy of colonialism or imperialism vis-a-vis Third World regions, with the exception of Asia. Japan is still perceived as being 'apolitical' in international behavior—that is, it projects an image of economic efficiency over political obtrusiveness, and of being less politically controversial, and less interventionist than other economic powers.

Furthermore, among other industrial powers, Japan occupies the unique position of belonging to both the Asian and Western blocs. In technological sophistication, economic power, and democratic behavior, Japan is a part of the West, but a part of Asia in terms of geographic location, proximity to other Asian nations, and the historical legacy manifested in its past involvements in Asia. The countries in the region, China, South Korea, and the NICs as well as the ASEAN and South Pacific nations are increasingly becoming strategic in Japan's security calculations, motivated by the changing global economic and military contexts. South Korea, although a NIC, still receives substantial Japanese development aid. Its most recent attention in aid-giving behavior focused on the South Pacific nations where it has increased economic assistance. Five principles of Japanese policy towards these nations were announced in 1987 with the visit of Foreign Minister Kuranaic Tadashi. This expression of political interest in the region had a strong dosage of foreign aid as an instrument to enhance regional cooperation and maintain regional stability. Between 1985 and 1987 Japanese ODA funds jumped from $24 million to $68 million, more than one percent of the total ODA.[2]

In aid, trade and investment the region of Asia takes priority in Japan's global and regional economic calculations. For example, the top ten recipients of Japan's bilateral aid are virtually all concentrated in the Asian region. For five consecutive years (1982–1986) they included almost the same recipients: China, Thailand, Philippines, Indonesia, Burma, Malaysia, Bangladesh, Pakistan, Sri Lanka, India, and Egypt. In terms of Japan's aid distribution, the Asian region can be divided into three sub-regions: Northeast Asia, Southeast Asia, and Southwest Asia. Almost all Japanese aid to Northeast Asia since 1982 is extended to China. Aid to China surpasses even aid to individual ASEAN members (Thailand, Indonesia, Singapore, the Philippines, Malaysia, and Brunei) in South east Asia. In Japan's aid policies ASEAN nations are always given priority with each major decision sensitive to possible ASEAN reaction. Of the three subregions, Southwest Asian countries receive the smallest share of Japanese aid. They include countries such as Pakistan, India, Sri Lanka, Burma, and Bangladesh.

On the whole, in Japanese regional aid distribution, Asian nations are the focus of a "differentiated approach"—that is they receive special treatment by way of aid concentration because in Japanese official parlance, "Asian nations have substantial financial needs in order to develop and Japan has had close historic, political and economic relations with the region."[3] The region still receives between 65 percent and 70 percent of all Japanese bilateral assistance. The concentration on Asian nations is also due to the U.S. pressures on Japan to assume, more responsibilities for development and regional stability following its own withdrawal from Vietnam in 1975. For example, the August 1977 Fukuda Doctrine promising to focus greater attention on ASEAN countries marked a redefinition of economic cooperation partly resulting from U.S. pressure. By the end of the 1970s a 7-1-1-1 formula became the guiding rule of Japanese regional distribution of aid. It means approximately 70 percent of total aid went to Asia, with Africa, Latin America and Middle East receiving roughly 10 percent each.[4] The continued diversification in aid distribution will no doubt change this ratio but for now Asia continues to be by far the foremost recipient of Japan's aid because of obvious historic, political, economic and geographic reasons.

With the end of the postwar reparations agreement between Japan and the ASEAN countries, a new relationship was entered into underpinned by economic cooperation. In addition, the first oil crisis of 1973—an event of profound global change—jolted Japan out of its aloof attitude towards the Third World. The strategic position of developing regions over access to critical raw materials was quickly realized. Apart from the maintenance of peaceful relationships the importance of enhancing political stability in strategic countries also became a concern of Japan. Foreign aid was viewed as a principal vehicle that could guarantee stability and peaceful relations with Japan and in turn provide access to markets, resources, and investment outlets. Japan thus broadened its foreign policy focus and shifted from a policy of detachment to one of internationalization. The diversification that came along with the increased external involvement would decrease dependence on a few suppliers. The enormous growth in the foreign aid budget since 1986 is mostly made up of funds from Japan's trade surplus controlled largely by the business sector. Trade, in other words, tends to enhance aid-giving, just as aid follows the flag in relationships between major industrial powers and developing countries.

Japan could be said to be shaping the Asian region into what is increasingly being referred to as an Asian "global buying network"—opening up of subsidiaries in Asia, production of parts rather than just finished products; in short a marked increased in intra-ASEAN trade. With these developments, there is emerging as noted by MITI, a "growing tendency for Japanese industry, especially the electrical machinery industry, to view the Pacific region as a single market from which to pursue a global corporate strategy."[5] For example, in December 1987, Prime Minister Takeshita announced during his visit to Manila the launch of a $2 billion development fund to promote small and medium-sized businesses in the Asian region.

Within Asia, Japan's trade expansion has been motivated by China's economic reforms and the rise of the "Four Tigers"—South Korea, Hong Kong, Taiwan and Singapore. This regional trade expansion has nonetheless been at the expense of trade with Africa and Latin America in particular. In the areas of trade, foreign direct investments and foreign aid, Japan's relationship with ASEAN has also strengthened over the past three years. Japan traditionally purchases large amounts of mineral fuels, crude oil and petroleum, refined oil products and liquefied methane gas from these countries such that it traditionally has run a large trade deficit with the six countries. The main source of tension in Japan-ASEAN trade relations revolves around the composition of Japan's imports from the region. ASEAN officials frequently charge that Japan continues to view the six-nation group merely as a source of agricultural commodities and industrial inputs rather than as a producer of equally valuable manufactured products. In 1987, for example, manufactures amounted to just 16.8 percent of Japanese purchases from ASEAN out of an overall import ratio of 40.5 percent.[6] The composition of Japan's imports from the group in relation to the composition of its exports to the group reflect the traditional pattern of North-South trade relations. Machinery and transport equipment, metals, chemical, textiles, and nonmetallic mineral products, among others, constitute exports to ASEAN, whereas imports include mostly mineral fuels, food, ores and scrap, and other raw materials. Similar to foreign aid distribution to Third World regions, Japan's regional trade is dominated by Asia. Imports in particular come predominantly from Pacific Basin nations and Asian nations. Asia's share of total imports rose sharply in the mid 1970s to early 1980s, a time when the yen was yet relatively weak in relation to the dollar and to most Asian currencies pegged to the dollar.

Similarly, in Japanese direct foreign investments to developing regions, Asia has primarily occupied first place in relation to Latin America, the Middle East and Africa. The growing economic strength of the NICs—Taiwan, South Korea, Hong Kong, and Singapore in particular—is impelling Japanese companies to shift their labor-intensive assembly enterprises away to Southeast Asia. Japanese firms are also engaging in diversification of their foreign investments by relying on their overseas facilities to produce parts and assemble final products. In large part, the significant increase in the yen's value against the dollar, and competitive necessity, have driven Japanese firms to diversify regionally as well as product wise. Other reasons contributing to the global outlook of Japanese investments are first the availability of cheap labor in contrast to the shortages of labor in Japan. Second, is the shortage and consequent high cost of industrial sites in Japan. Third, is the effect of one of the 3 Es of the 1990s, the Environment, (the other two are Economy and Ethics). The increasing number of environmental laws and regulations is putting constraints on industrial activities. This is also related to the impact of economic nationalism in both developed and developing nations. Restrictions on the volume of Japanese exports in Third World countries are the key constraints in this area. Finally, the expanding global focus of Japanese investment is due to easier access to industrial inputs and lower electricity costs for energy-intensive products.

The prominent role of Asia in Japanese investments is related to the existence of NICs like Singapore or Hong Kong which until the mid 1980s were the preferred locations for Japan's overseas production ventures. Their attractiveness was due to low labor costs, relative political stability, geographic and cultural proximity to Japan, and an open door policy with regards to direct foreign investments. These are key factors that inspire extremely high levels of confidence on those countries among Japanese investors. However, one of the global changes that is currently affecting Japanese direct foreign investments is the diminished economic advantages of the "four tigers" as they mature into Newly Industrializing Status. Concrete examples of their growing economic power are the rising value of the Korean and Taiwanese currencies vis-a-vis the dollar, reducing the cost advantages of producing in these countries for shipment back to Japan or the United States. In other words, the NICs of Asia are no longer low-cost hosts for labor-intensive goods like textiles that Japanese firms traditionally have produced there.

The need for Japan to shift production away from the NICs is also due to the fact that the U.S. has withdrawn its Generalized System of Preferences (GSP) from them because of the trade deficits it is running with all four ($9.9 billion, $14.1 billion, $2.5 billion, and $5.1 billion with South Korea, Taiwan, Singapore, and Hong Kong respectively in 1988).[7] This means that a significant amount of Japanese products made in the NICs traditionally have been exported to the U.S. as a third market. The opening up of new offshore sourcing locations thus becomes a necessity for Japan's economic security to use them as a location from which to supply the U.S. market until they also "graduate" from the American GSP. The Asian NICs in turn are being considered for a new role in Japan's global economic policy—locations for higher technology investments. This is in addition to cooperative ventures between Japanese firms and NICs in the areas of hotels, retail outlets and wholesale distribution, financial services and other industries that depend on the patronage of NIC nationals.

The geographic shift in the production of lower cost goods for export is increasingly toward some ASEAN members. Malaysia, Thailand, Indonesia, and the Philippines are primary targets of this trend because of their low investment costs and very attractive exchange rates compared to NICs in the region. Already, they are among the major locations of Japan's foreign direct investments with Indonesia the recipient of up to $9,804 million in investments in March 1989, and the Philippines, the smallest amount, up to $1,120 million.[8] In terms of investment attractiveness, South Asia is also in the same category as Southeast Asia, although investment in that region is still very small. India, however, will continue to be promising and very attractive because of low wages and stability.

The geographic diversification of investments, of course, also involves political stability considerations. Each country within a region has its own advantages and disadvantages, as well as its own local laws or regulations concerning direct foreign investments. Overall, political uncertainties have had little effect on investment in Asian NICs, even though Hong Kong and South Korea are not immune from such political considerations. For example, what changes will Beijing introduce into the current capitalist economic structure of Hong Kong after 1997? South Korea is not immune from periodic labor and radical student unrest.

Japanese investment expansion into other regions is also susceptible to other political uncertainties like the instability generated by the Iran-Iraq War, or the volatility of the recent Iraqi occupation of Kuwait. Nationalization of foreign companies, physical damage to the facility or changes in the host government's attitudes toward investment are the resulting factors from political instability.

Another factor of importance to Japan's investment globalism in particular, is fear of growing "Japanophobia" because of a significant Japanese industrial presence in a country. An example was the anti-Japanese riots in Bangkok and Jakarta in 1974. Also of relevance are stiff investment requirements and laws including regulations governing export performance, local ownership, and local content. Finally, there are the increasing international criticisms regarding the effects of Japanese investment practices on the global environment, one of the 3 Es of the 1990s. For example, concern over the degradation of the rain forests in Indonesia and Brazil are manifestations of this environmental issue. Overall, advanced industrial countries and NICs including Malaysia, Indonesia, and India inspire greater investment confidence in Japanese investors. However, many Third World countries fall into the considerable risk category.

Critics of Japan's economic expansionism point to a strong Japanese determination to consolidate its hold on the Asian region. This is manifested in a lust for Asian markets as part of the Japanese lust for global markets, new avenues of investment, and access to raw materials for its industries. A consequence of this corporate globalism is that Japanese economic behavior is at times basically structured by mixed motives. This trend is especially the pattern in the Asian region. In August 1990, a year after China crushed pro-democracy demonstrations in Tianamen Square, Japan took the lead in relaxing sanctions against China. This foreign policy behavior on the part of Japan could be interpreted as a mixture of: (1) concern for regional stability; (2) guilt about atrocities committed in World War II against China; and (3) a lust for global markets. According to Japanese officials, a resumption of the foreign aid relationship could help revive the sagging trade and rejuvenate the Chinese economy. Accordingly, Prime Minister Toshiki Kaifu announced in July 1990 that Japan will gradually restore a five-year package of loans worth 810 billion yen ($5.4 billion).[9] Prime Minister Kaifu defended his decision in terms of the need to maintain regional stability. Isolation of China, he argued, is counterproductive of regional stability.

In particular, the relaxation of sanctions, according to former Foreign Minister Saburo Okita is due to the fact that: "Japan invaded China and caused widespread death, destruction and devastation. Japanese feel guilt about China, not about the Soviet Union."[10] The Japanese find it difficult to continue protesting human rights violations either in China or other countries in the region that suffered from Japanese imperialism and cruelty during World War II. Japanese who favor relaxing sanctions argue that in the heydays of Japanese imperialism in China, more than 100,000 civilians and prisoners of war were slaughtered in Nanking (then capital of China) in late 1937, far more than the Chinese People's Liberation Army did on the night of June 3-4, 1989. Tokuma Utsunomiya, a member of the Japanese Diet and head of the Japan-China Friendship Society has emphasized that "Japan has a responsibility to help China's modernization," because of the ruthless and ruinous Japanese occupation.[11] With regard to economic expansion in particular, a Japan-China Investment Promotion Organization was formed in March 1990 with government support. It is argued in top echelons of the Japanese government and economic sectors, that aid, trade and investment links with China will help improve China's economy out of which democracy can then thrive.

In sum, Japan's restoration of economic cooperation (in particular foreign aid) links with China, underscores the significant role played by resource diplomacy in Japan's pursuit of comprehensive security and developmental goals in the Asian region. Foreign aid in particular articulates into Japan's Asian policy of building and maintaining cordial relations necessary for solid trade and investment activities.

Entanglements in the Middle East

As far as major powers are concerned, their level of political entanglements in a region is largely determined by the volatility and explosivity of prevalent regional issues. Ordinarily, the initial focus on sound economic relationships generates regional obligations that take the form of supporting one faction against another, even entering into military alliances, or protecting sources of strategic raw materials. Foreign economic activities are definitely also affected by the vicissitudes of global economic events often resulting in significant rearrangements of Japan's economic expansion. In trade, for example, the 1973–74 OPEC boost in crude oil prices tripled Japan's imports from the Middle East during that period, and they doubled again between 1978 and 1979. By 1987 the falling crude oil prices, and a stronger yen relative to dollar-denominated oil contracts, reduced imports.

In Japan's economic globalism, the Middle East, as a region, has particularly challenged Japan's adaptive skills in a changing international environment. Since 1973, the region, for the first time, formed a significant element of concern in Japanese foreign policy, and since then has assumed dramatic importance and demanded far more attention. In other words, the pattern of Japan's economic globalism entered a new stage with the oil crisis of the 1970s. In aid distribution, for example, globalism was extended beyond Asia to resource-endowed countries in other regions of the Third World. In the case of the Middle East, aid distribution is predicated more on comprehensive national security concerns—that is the linkage of both military and non-military factors (defense, energy and other noneconomic factors) in the disbursement of aid. Egypt is now among the top ten recipients of Japanese aid and Turkey was the recipient, on approval by Tokyo, of an Export-Import Bank/World Bank co-financed loan of $388.6 million.[12]

In Japan's global economic expansionism, the Middle East occupies a critical place because the region is the source of almost 70 percent of Japan's crude oil supplies. In security terms the region is therefore of strategic importance to Japan. Complicating the leverage that individual countries in the region could have on Japan's foreign policy are the sensitive issues of the Arab-Israeli conflict and U.S. foreign policy objectives in the region in general and its stance towards the Arab-Israeli (Palestinian) question. The aftermath of the 1973 Arab-Israeli war in particular forced Japan to assess its security and political strategies in the region. One consequence of the war was that Japan and other oil-importing nations were faced with the threat of an Arab oil embargo if their foreign policy was not deemed supportive of the Arab cause. Tokyo in 1973 found itself in a power-dependence dilemma. On the one hand, it needed and depended on oil deliveries to sustain the very foundation of its economy. On the other hand, Japan was almost a 'captive' and sympathetic to the U.S. firm support of Israel, as Japan is virtually a member of the Western military-security camp. This dimension of Japan's global security is analyzed further in Chapter Five.

Its real and potential dilemmas in the Middle East has impelled Tokyo to utilize foreign aid as a central vehicle in efforts to promote stability in the region. The underlying rationale for this strategy is that economic security is the most important factor in the guarantee of political stability. Japan's bilateral ODA to the region is in the neighborhood of 9 to 10 percent of its total annual disbursements. The aid has been targeted mostly at strategically located, moderate countries like Egypt, Pakistan, Turkey, Jordan, Yemen, Iraq, and Sudan. In 1986 Egypt was the tenth largest recipient of Japan's ODA totalling $126 million. Pakistan received an even larger amount, $152 million, making it the eighth largest recipient.[13] The motivation for the aid package to Pakistan was its proximity to the Afghanistan civil war. The profile of countries receiving most Japanese economic assistance strongly indicates that while Tokyo does not extend military aid, it nonetheless increases economic aid to countries that are strategic to the Western alliance. Economic aid to the region is also predicated on the maintenance of friendly political relations with major oil suppliers like Saudi Arabia which in 1986 received $14.5 million.[14] Apart from strategic and economic concerns, aid is also extended for specific problems such as disaster relief funds for Lebanon. However, the Japanese aid efforts in the Middle East need not be overstated. In comparative terms proportionally more aid has been extended to Sub-Saharan Africa than to the Middle East. One obstacle working against increased aid flows to the region is, of course, the higher income status of countries in the region which makes them ineligible for Japan's ODA.

In the area of trade, Japan's new globalism with regards to the Middle East could be traced as far back as the 1950s when she intensified her search for new markets in areas distant from the Pacific Basin. The Middle Eastern countries established relations with Japan with little difficulty because they had not suffered the brunt of Japanese military power. Sales offices were opened in key Middle Eastern cities—Cairo, Beirut, Tehran, among others. Sales of Japanese machinery in the region multiplied 8.5 times between 1955 and 1965: from $10 million to $85 million. By the end of 1972, sales increased five times more to $400 million.[15] Even before World War II, Japan was a major source of inexpensive consumer goods for many Middle Eastern countries, particularly Iran and Iraq. With the post World War II period, Japan became both a heavy exporter of commodities like textiles, machinery and plant equipment, and the single largest importer of Persian Gulf oil.

Prior to the recent Persian Gulf crisis, Japan's annual trade with the Middle East surpassed the $60 billion mark, with roughly two-thirds of that amount accounted for by its strong dependence on oil imports that are critical to its economic viability. This significant dependence on oil from the region was impressed upon the Japanese during the 1973 Yom Kippur War.[16] Perhaps for the first time the Japanese were vividly made to realize that politics, to use Marxian logic, is the superstructure that perennially hangs over the base of economic activities. Because of its economic vulnerability, Japan was at a disadvantage in the power politics of the October 1973 Arab-Israeli War. It had to declare its support of Palestinian self-determination and called on Israel to hand back the territories it occupied since the 1967 Arab-Israeli conflict. The reciprocal response of the Arab nations was to accord Japan "friendly nation" status with the assurance of an uninterrupted flow of oil.

The power politics of Japan's oil vulnerability to the Middle East is reflected in its moderate policies toward Iran and the PLO, in contrast to what Japan considers overly hostile U.S. policies toward the PLO. Japan allowed the PLO to open an office in Tokyo, and Prime Minister Suzuki met in a "nonofficial capacity" with Yasir Arafat. The power politics of oil dependence creates a security policy divergence with the U.S. since Washington has refused to recognize the PLO or push hard for a Palestinian homeland. A confluence of security interests results in policy similarities, while divergent U.S. and Japanese interests produce regional policy differences. During the recent Persian Gulf crisis, Japan was not presented with a security dilemma similar to 1973 because an overwhelming number of Arab states were on the side of the U.S. and European Community members. It was easier for Japan to maintain its solidarity with the West and its autonomy, while at the same time finding security in numbers. In this instance, solidarity with the U.S. and its own national interests were not conflictual and full of tensions. In other words, Japan's trade dilemmas in the Middle East are better solved by a divided Arab world and the diminished power of OPEC in the global politics of oil. Arab unity and escalating tensions over the Arab-Israeli question could again propel Japan into a security dilemma reminiscent of 1973 in which it would be forced to take sides, and most likely dissociate itself from U.S. policies in the region.

In the Middle East as in other developing regions, foreign direct investments constitute one of the components of Japan's three-pronged approach to economic cooperation with other nations. By March 1989 Japan's investments in the region had reached $3,338 million.[17] The chemical, mining, and insurance industries comprise the most important in terms of amount of money invested. Next in importance are the metals and construction industries. The overwhelming dependence on oil and the region's oil supplies has led some firms to invest in oil related ventures, such that by March 1989, Japan had up to 1,389 branch offices throughout the region.[18] Ordinarily, Japan's strategy of strengthening political ties with oil-rich Middle Eastern countries is through large-scale investments such as the multi-million dollar petrochemical complex in Saudi Arabia run by Mitsubishi. Japan's involvement in the region has been dramatic since the October 1973 War. A concrete example of global involvement in non-economic issues was the 1983 diplomatic initiative launched by Foreign Minister Abe to convince Iran and Iraq to discontinue their war. The same year Japan offered to fund an expanded multinational force for Lebanon along with involvement in other United Nations peacekeeping activities in the region.[19] In investments, Japanese firms in the construction and petrochemicals sectors pervade the Middle East today. However, compared to the Asian region, investments have received little attention as yet. Political instability, and cultural distance are considered impediments to

Japanese investments in the region. Shipping registration activities and resource-extraction operations have so far largely been the focus. Instability has tended, and will continue, to undermine the attractiveness of the region.

Africa and Latin America: Emerging Horizons

The economic superpower status of Japan, its role as the largest world creditor, and the external pressures on it to play a more constructive role in the international system has produced in Japan an obsession with global image that is continually on the increase. In June 19–24, 1988, at the Toronto economic summit of advanced industrial countries, Prime Minister Noboru Takeshita underscored Japan's commitment to help in resolving the economic problems of the Third World. Accordingly, he proposed no less than three initiatives at the summit, indicating Japan's willingness to become more active in policymaking instead of its usual pattern of merely following the U.S. in policy formulation. The aid doubling plan constitutes Japan's first initiative, a pledge to disburse $50 billion in ODA during the 1988–92 period. The second initiative comprised of a $5.5 billion debt relief package specifically for 17 least developed nations in Africa and Asia.[20]

The global dimensions of Japan's economic expansionism, when viewed regionally, have been uneven. In investments, for example, more Japanese direct foreign investments are still concentrated in the U.S. and Europe for both strategic, political and long-term reasons. In Europe in particular, the Japanese objective is to establish a presence in order to be counted as a local producer in anticipation of the possibility of expanded local content laws and regulations and as the possibility of increased economic nationalism looms larger in the 1990s.[21] In the Third World, Asia has been the key recipient of Japanese investments. This is related to the existence of NICs like Singapore or Hong Kong which until the mid 1980s were the preferred locations for Japan's overseas production ventures. While Africa and Latin America are still relegated to a secondary role in Japan's economic globalism, they are steadily being incorporated through the instrumentality of foreign aid in particular. For example, in addition to the top ten Japanese aid recipients concentrated in the Asian region, Japan also extends aid to various other countries, including, for example, in 1987, Syria ($45.07 million); Sudan ($77.70 million); Zambia ($41.68 million); Tanzania ($46.04 million); Malawi

($51.52 million); Ecuador ($46.06 million); Paraguay ($39.28 million); and Peru ($37.55 million).[22]

Japan's growing foreign aid distribution to Third World regions has been motivated by the realization that increasing violence and conflicts in developing countries threaten their capacity to be reliable sources of raw materials, stable markets for finished goods, and attractive avenues of new direct foreign investments. Accordingly, economic aid is viewed by Japan as an effective vehicle to the maintenance of a peaceful global economic system and in particular stable regional economic systems. This objective of foreign aid—the maintenance of political stability in specific countries—has given Japanese aid the character of a differentiated approach: that is aid being concentrated on countries of most strategic importance to Japan. Sometimes referred to as 'strategic aid', it has been extended since the 1970s in significant amounts to countries as far apart from each other as Pakistan, Zimbabwe, Jamaica, Turkey, Egypt, Kenya, North Yemen, Somalia, and Sudan, in addition to China, South Korea and the ASEAN countries.

Since the 1970s Japan's economic aid has also been used to specifically influence regional political outcomes. It was used as a means of applying sanctions against Vietnam, Kampuchea, Cuba, Angola, Afghanistan, and Ethiopia. Japan has also used aid as a political tool in the Philippines with the emergence of the Aquino regime, and in Afghanistan after the Soviet pull out. In Burma aid has been extended as a means of encouragement for the nation to abandon its autarkic economic policy and adopt a more open orientation in foreign economic relations.

In response to criticisms of its foreign aid distribution program, the Japanese government announced in 1986 its intention to distribute worldwide $20 billion in ODA mainly through multilateral aid agencies. In 1987 another $20 billion was added to the amount, and in June 1988 the fourth "doubling plan" for aid since 1978 was announced with a promise at a target of $50 billion during the period 1988–92. Sub-Saharan Africa which in the past and even now has figured least in Japanese aid, trade, investment and overall security calculations was promised a $500 million aid package over a three-year period from 1987.[23] As reflected in its selective approach to aid-giving, Japan has emphasized economic self-interest over African political issues, even over those touching on "liberation." Aid and trade are thus closely interrelated in Japan's economic expansion to Africa because of the attitude of viewing Africa as merely a source of natural resources in Japan's economic behavior in the region.

Aid distribution which correlates strongly with trade patterns in the region is focused largely on significant economic partners, in particular suppliers of raw materials. Kenya, Madagascar, Niger, Sudan, Tanzania, Zaire, and Zambia, are among the handful of favored countries. This pattern could be traced back to the 1960s and has not changed much since. The least developed countries of Africa, such as Burkina Faso, Mali, Niger, and Chad, among others have been largely neglected. The new global orientation of Japan since the early 1970s did not significantly affect its relationship with the continent. Japan is still inclined to separate economics from politics in relation to African issues. With the Fukuda doctrine declared on August 1975, the Committee on Foreign Economic Cooperation advocated the establishment of a more effective pattern of resource diplomacy structured by increased economic cooperation and grant aid. As a consequence, Japan's ODA increased by 55 percent in 1977, by 19 percent in 1979, and by 16 percent in 1980.[24] The increase to Africa was almost twofold from 1977 to 1978, but fell again in 1981.

In Africa, it is in the area of trade that Japan's economic globalism intersects with political realities—in particular with South African apartheid. The policy of diversifying its foreign relations in the mid 1970s seemed to have changed Japan's attitude toward Africa from negative to positive. This change of attitude was manifested first in its June 1974 public announcement of the suspension of sports, cultural, and educational interchanges with South Africa. Second, Japan made some initial moves of trade restrictions with South Africa and awarded diplomatic recognition to Guinea Bissau on August, 1974. Japan had previously abstained from voting in the United Nations General Assembly in November, 1973 on a resolution advocating recognition to the independence of Guinea Bissau. Third, the then foreign minister, Toshio Kimura, made an official visit to Ghana, Nigeria, and Tanzania between October and November of 1974. It marked the first visit ever to Africa by a Japanese foreign minister. This new diplomacy subsided again after 1975. In 1979 it picked up again when Sunao Sonoda, as foreign minister, made visits to Nigeria, Ivory Coast, Senegal, Tanzania and Kenya.[25] The visits, according to observers, were motivated by the desire to secure access to raw materials because Japan faced another oil crisis in 1979 and was making efforts to reduce its dependence on Middle Eastern oil and gas. Its attack on the apartheid system was not sustained because Japan consistently increased the trade between it and South Africa while still formally condemning racism and apartheid in Africa.

Trade with Africa reflects the North-South structure of economic relations in which Japan exports industrial manufactures and imports raw materials. The trade pattern is basically asymmetrical with metal goods, textiles, synthetic fibers and machinery making up the Japanese exports, while fiber, iron ore, crude oil, and foods mostly make up the imported items from Africa. In addition to the vertical and unbalanced structure of trade, the trading partners were limited to countries with natural resources needed by Japan.[26] As in the case of South Africa, Japan was inclined to trade with such countries regardless of their domestic political problems or of whether a great deal of world wide criticism was directed against them. With South Africa, for example, before 1989 the Japanese government adopted an attitude of indifference toward UN resolutions calling for sanctions against South Africa. Japanese trade substantially increased to the extent that South Africa ranked first among Japan's African trading partners. The main reason for trading with South Africa seems to be the availability of many important resources not easily obtainable elsewhere and of better access to a market for Japanese goods than in other countries.

Japan's stubborn tendency to ignore the apartheid issue in its economic relations with South Africa prompted U.S. Representative Mervyn Dymally to issue an eleven point statement in October 1988 calling on Japanese companies to end trade with South Africa and for Japan to adopt a more satisfactory conduct in international interracial relations.[27] The appreciation of the yen was partly responsible for Japan becoming South Africa's leading trade partner. Besides, Japanese companies seemed to have stepped in when U.S. companies withdrew from South Africa.

The pressure on Japan reached its highest point on December 6, 1988, when the UN General Assembly passed a resolution calling for a ban on trade with South Africa in which it explicitly criticized Japan for taking over the number one trading partner position with the apartheid regime. It was the first time that Tokyo was singled out for criticism in the organization since it became a member in 1956. Just as it is vulnerable to the politics in the Arab-Israeli conflict, so also is Japan vulnerable to the politics involved in trade with Pretoria. Japan, in other words, is increasingly realizing that in some Third World regions, it is not possible to separate economics from politics.

The UN criticism elicited responses in Japanese domestic politics. The Chairman of the Japan Socialist Party, Takako Doi, called on Tokyo to impose comprehensive economic sanctions against South Africa and cease from being a human rights midget.[28] By the end of January 1989, Japan was no longer South Africa's leading trade partner. Trade between the two countries declined 3.5 percent during 1988, yielding first position to West Germany.[29] The UN resolution and international criticism affected Japan's trading behavior, although ANC representatives argue that Japan has not done enough compared to other nations like Sweden or New Zealand.

During the yen's steep climb, many of Japan's private-sector companies moved quickly to internationalize their operations and also joined U.S. companies in developing an international division of labor that took advantage of market mechanisms and involved the Asia-Pacific region. Even at the governmental level, the African continent had received little consideration from Japan until the oil crisis. Japan's efforts to improve relations with countries in the region are still largely in the area of trade. Until recently, in the foreign aid area, aid was often provided for infrastructural projects whose aim was to facilitate the export of primary products. This included mostly the period prior to 1973 when the so-called tied aid idea linked aid to the promotion of internal industries. The beginnings of investment operations are currently manifested, as in Latin America, in shipping registration activities and resource-extraction operations.

Observers argue that the principal impediments to Japanese economic expansion in the region are: cultural diversity, geographic distance, and in particular political instability. However, between 1951 and 1982, Japan had over 700 different ventures in sub-Saharan Africa worth over $2 billion. The amount is small compared to Japanese direct investments in other regions because it represented only 4.4 percent of total Japanese direct foreign investments. Asia, Latin America, and the Middle East with 29 percent, 16.2 percent, and 5.2 percent respectively attracted far more Japanese investments than Africa.[30] Again, Africa has not been very attractive because of the general lack of historical ties between the two regions, ignorance of Japanese firms about Africa, and the overall impression that has been fostered that Africa is a bad risk.

On the whole, the current money value of Japanese direct foreign investments in Africa reveal fluctuating trends. Between 1984 and 1989 the trend was as follows: from $326 million in 1984 the value of investments decreased to $172 million in 1985; it was on the upswing again in 1986 at $309 million followed by a downswing in 1987 at $272 million. The values for 1988 and 1989 show a significant increase of \$653 million and \$4,604 million respectively.[31] In the manufacturing sector, the emphasis is placed on textiles, chemicals, metals, and transport equipment; whereas in the nonmanufacturing sector, the focus is on fisheries, mining, services transportation, and real estate.

The pattern and scope of Japanese investments in the region are undergoing change characterized by partnership with African interests. With the 1973 oil crisis there has been investment expansion toward the development of stable sources of raw materials, more regional involvement focusing on local manufacturing in which African countries involve more Japanese participation. The investment emphasis, in other words, has diversified from the previous sole emphasis on ship leasing and other maritime enterprises, mining and vehicle assembly to local manufacturing based on partnership with African interests.

In addition to the growing importance of the Middle East to Japan, Latin America has assumed a new significance for Tokyo's policymakers. Prime Ministers Tanaka and Ohira both visited the region in pursuit of oil and other raw materials, and Japan has entered into economic cooperation agreements with Brazil. Japan's efforts to diversify its diplomacy were an expression of a sense of crisis prevalent among the Japanese in the mid-1970s, and the policy of diversifying foreign relations seemed to attain success to some degree.

In its obsession with globalism, Japan is even quite willing to capitalize on the election in June 1990 of Japanese descendant Alberto Fujimori as president of Peru. The newly-elected president was given a hero's welcome amid the groundswell of national pride the Japanese expressed in the overseas success of a native son. Japan provided Peru with \$145 million foreign aid—grants, technical assistance and low-interest loans—from 1984 to 1988. In 1989, though, Japan cut off its low-interest loans to Peru after Peru defaulted on parts of its \$15 billion in foreign debt.[32] The ethnic connection with the new Peruvian president will undoubtedly encourage Japan to reassess its economic ties with Peru and perhaps provide it with foreign aid and investments. Generally, Japan's ties with Latin America have been weak, with the notable exception of Brazil. Just as in Peru, ethnicity also links the two countries together and is manifested in the approximately 1.2 million people of Japanese descent in Brazil.

In Latin America, Brazil, Mexico, Bolivia, Paraguay, Peru, and Honduras are among the top recipients of Japan's foreign aid. However, the ever shrinking U.S. foreign aid to the region assures greater significance in terms of security concerns when viewed in the context of the region's debt crisis, drug wars, civil wars, and poverty. The U.S. is undoubtedly looking forward to a greater Japanese role in the region in the face of the magnitude of problems. In 1990, for example, Japan pledged to provide economic assistance to Panama, whose economy was devastated by the U.S.-Noriega conflict that resulted in Washington imposing economic sanctions on Panama and invading the country to force Noriega out of power and to install a pro-U.S. regime. In addition, Tokyo also pledged to give assistance to Nicaragua following the defeat of the Sandanistas in the 1990 presidential election. In such instances of U.S.-Japan interface of political and economic roles, we see the beginnings of a mutual readiness to engage in more constructive collaborations in Third World development problems.

Analyzed by country, the most important for Japan as an export market is apparently Panama, which absorbed 21 percent of the total Japanese exports to Latin America in 1981. The highest percentage for Panama is due to imports from Japan that consist mainly of ships with flags of convenience. In other words, a large part of Japanese exports to Panama cannot actually be considered exports to that country. Mexico and Brazil constituted the second and third markets for Japan, having 16.2 and 13.0 percent of total exports respectively.[33] They were followed by Andean countries such as Venezuela, Chile, and Colombia, as well as Argentina. Generally, in trade, Japan has had a constant trade deficit with the region, totalling $3 billion in 1989 because of Japan's need for agricultural and energy-intensive products.

For some countries in the region, Japanese direct investment account for a high proportion of the total foreign direct investments. In Mexico, for example, the direct foreign investments from Japan amounted to about $500 million toward the end of 1980, accounting for approximately 6 percent of the total foreign investments in Mexico. In Brazil, it was $1.518 billion, accounting for 9.5 percent of the total foreign investments in Brazil in 1979.[34] Latin America is in fact second in terms of Japanese concentration of investments in Third World regions. Between FY 1985 and FY 1988 investments in the region more than doubled. But only 17 percent of Japanese investments in the region is focused on the manufacturing sector.[35] A substantial part of the remainder is what has been referred to as "paper investment," and also includes shipping registration in, for example, Panama, Increased stability in Central and South America coupled with more European and North American economic integration is bound to attract more Japanese economic activities to the region as a whole.

Summary

In Japan's push for economic globalism, foreign assistance articulates into the North-South policy of building and maintaining cordial relations with LDCs. Resource diplomacy as expressed in foreign aid promotes interdependence and its underlying factors of access to raw materials, markets, and investment avenues. One of the imperatives of economic globalism is that at times Japan is caught between a two-way power-dependence: on the one hand, is its close ties with the United States, and on the other hand, is its need to strengthen political ties with oil-rich nations even in the face of policy divergence with the United States. In its economic security dilemmas in the Middle East—the 1973–74 Arab oil embargo, the 1980 Iranian hostage crisis, and the Iran-Iraq War, to name a few—Japan's dependence on the oil-rich nations assumes a more vulnerable character, than its dependence on United States protection of commercial sea lanes. Thus its failure to always reciprocate United States initiatives in the region. In other words, while U.S.-Japan economic security considerations tend to converge in the Asian region, in the Middle East because of Japan's vulnerability to Arab oil power politics they clearly diverge on many issues largely underpinned by the Arab-Israeli conflict.

In economic matters, Japan's image has undergone tremendous change toward a more prestigious international position. But Japan's economic ascendancy commands more attention because of the corresponding relative economic decline of the United States. As early as 1982 the United States was the world's largest creditor but by 1987 it had been replaced by Japan. The change in Japan's global economic projection in the areas of aid, trade and investment is of very recent vintage because even after it became a global economic power in the 1970s its aid, trade and investment position was still regionally-focused and less diversified. This three-pronged economic expansion strategy of aid, trade and investment which is the cornerstone of Japan's new globalism, has also been extended to the regions of Africa and Latin America.

It is in Japan's economic globalism that the complexity of interdependence is noticeably manifested. Economic expansionism tends to intersect conflictually with political realities creating dilemmas for Japan. Or bilateral U.S.-Japan relationships tend to manifest themselves in constructive collaboration efforts of mutual benefit as in Japan's complementary role in Panama, Nicaragua, or the Philippines. Besides, a balancing act to pursue economic objectives and at the same time avoid being entangled in regional conflicts is now an integral part of Japan's foreign economic policy in the developing regions of Asia, Africa, Latin America, and the Middle East, regions which at times constitute a conundrum of numerous and seemingly intractable conflict situations. Finally, in its globalist orientation, economic security, comprehensive national security, omnidirectional diplomacy, and internationalization have all become a part of the parlance of Japan's foreign policy as it copes with a constantly changing international environment where it has become both a subject and an object of adaptation to accommodate to new realities.

Endnotes

1 Many works have either specifically focused upon, or made passing reference to, Japan's changing role in the international system, among them are: Ardath W. Burks, *Japan: A Postindustrial Power* (Boulder: Westview Press, 1984); Masatoka Kosaka (ed.) *Japan's Choices, New Globalism and Cultural Orientations in an Industrial State* (London: Pinter Publishers, 1989); Syed Jaaved Maswood, *Japan and Protection, The growth of protectionist sentiment and the Japanese response* (London: Routledge, 1989); and Takashi Inoguchi and Daniel Okimoto (eds.) *The Political Economy of Japan, Vol 2, The Changing International Contest* (Stanford: Stanford University Press, 1988).

2 *Japan's ODA 1988 Annual Report* (Tokyo: Ministry of Foreign Affairs) p. 45.

3 *Japan's ODA 1988 Annual Report*, p. 44.

4 See, *Japan Economic Institute (JEI) Report*, No. 43A (by Gretchen Green), November 11, 1988, p. 2.

5 *JEI Report*, No. 31A (by Eileen M. Doherty), August 11, 1989, p. 2.

6 *JEI Report*, No. 1A (by Gretchen Green), January 6, 1989, p. 3.

7 For further details, see, *JEI Report*, No. 31A, p. 7.

8 *Japan's Foreign Direct Investment, 1988 Annual Report* (Tokyo: Ministry of Finance), p. 15.

9 *International Herald Tribune*, August 1990, p. 20.

10 Dan Biers, "Japan leads rush to normalize relations with China," *The Tampa Tribune-Times*, August 19, 1990, p. 17-A.

11 Dan Briers, "Japan leads rush to normalize relations with China," p. 17-A.

12 See, for example, *Japan's ODA 1988 Annual Report*, pp. 44–46; and *JEI Report*, No. 41A (by Eileen Doherty), October 30, 1987, p. 12.

13 *Japan's ODA 1988 Annual Report*, p. 46.

14 *JEI Report*, No. 9A (by Eileen Doherty), March 4, 1988, p. 9.

15 See, Japan External Trade Organization (JETRO), *Foreign Trade of Japan*, annual volumes, 1955–1973 series.

16 For a detailed discussion of Japan's dilemma in the Arab-Israeli conflict, see

Michael M. Yoshitsu, *Caught in the Middle East* (Toronto: Lexington Books, 1984).

17 *JEI Report*, No. 31A (by Eileen Doherty), August 11, 1989, p. 4.

18 Ministry of Finance, *Japan's Foreign Direct Investment by Industry and Region*, Tokyo, March 31, 1989.

19 *Asahi Jaanaru*, August 8, 1984.

20 See, for example, *JEI Report*, No. 41A (by Gretchen Green), October 27, 1989, p. 2; and *Japan's ODA 1988 Annual Report*, pp. 6–7.

21 For further details on Japan's reactions to West European integration in 1992, see, Kenjiro Ishikawa, *Japan and the Challenge of Europe 1992* (London: Pinter Publishers, 1990).

22 *Japan's ODA 1988 Annual Report*, pp. 117–245.

23 For more details see, *JEI Report*, No. 20A (by Eileen Doherty), May 20, 1988, pp. 4–5.

24 Ministry of Foreign Affairs, *Diplomacy Blue Book*, 1975–1983.

25 For further details on Japan's economic objectives in Africa, see Hideo Oda and Kazuyoski Aoki, "Japan and Africa: Beyond the Fragile Partnership," in Robert S. Ozaki and Walter Arnold (eds.) *Japan's Foreign Relation: A Global Search for Economic Security* (Boulder: Westview Press, 1985) pp. 153–168.

26 For details on figures and countries, see, Ministry of Foreign Affairs, *Diplomacy Blue Book*, 1983.

27 See, for example, *JEI Report*, No. 42B (by Susan MacKnight), November 4, 1988, pp. 7–9.

28 *JEI Report*, No. 47B (by Gretchen Green), December 16, 1988, pp. 10–11.

29 *JEI Report*, No. 4B, January 27, 1989, p. 7.

30 David Morris, "Japanese Investment in Africa," *New African*, May 1983, p. 39; and *Africa Economic Digest*, 10 December 1982, p. 13.

31 *JEI Report*, No. 31A (by Eileen Doherty), August 11, 1989, p. 3; and Ministry of Finance, *Japan's Foreign Direct Investment by Country, FY 1984–FY 1988*.

32 Bob Dean's, "New President of Peru a source of pride in Japan," *Tampa Tribune-Times*, Sunday June 17, 1990, p. 8-A.

33 See, for example, MITI, *Present Situation and Problems of Economic Cooperation, 1982.*

34 MITI, *Present Situation and Problems of Economic Cooperation, 1982.*

35 *JEI Report*, No. 15A (by Gretchen Green), April 13, 1990, pp. 2–3.

3

JAPANESE FOREIGN AID AND THE GLOBAL AGENDA

Along with the demise of the Cold War, the growing momentum for West European economic integration, and the relative hegemonic decline of the United States, the other extraordinary development in international political economy during the last decade has been the global economic preeminence of Japan. In pure financial terms, there has already occurred a significant reversal of the financial positions of the United States and Japan such that the latter is now considered the main underwriter of what is left of American hegemony. This profound economic development has transformed the foreign policy orientation of Japan, modified the American-Japanese relationship, and is actively redefining Japan's role in the Third World agenda of issues.

Just as the United States had supplanted Great Britain during the interwar period as the world's principal creditor nation, so also did Japan displace the United States in the 1980s as the foremost creditor nation. Within the United States, more than 20 percent of all credit in the state of California is supplied by Japanese and Japanese-owned banks. In 1981, Japan became the world's foremost capital exporter such that by 1986 its net assets abroad had jumped to $129.8 billion from a figure of only $17.7 in 1983. Nine out of the world's ten largest banks are Japanese.[1] Since the mid 1980s, Japan had taken over the position of America's principal economic ally, a position once held by West Germany. This profound growth in Japan's overall economic power had begun in the first half of the 1970s mainly as a result of responses to the OPEC oil policies. In the area of foreign trade, Japan expanded its exports to earn more foreign exchange to pay for the high cost of oil, and it significantly reduced its energy consumption. These steps, coupled with several other important features of the Japanese political economy resulted in massive trade and payments surplus for the country.

Through a focused and multidimensional analysis of the Japanese foreign aid program it is possible to enhance understanding of how foreign aid has articulated into Japan's foreign economic objectives since the 1970s. The insights gained here will be applied to subsequent discussions of specific issues such as the debt problem, oil-politics, or apartheid in Japan's globalist orientation. This chapter will therefore focus on a broad range of questions such as: what role does foreign aid play in the global power economic behavior of Japan and in the United States-Japan bilateral relationship? Is the Japanese foreign aid program a foreign policy objective per se? How has foreign aid articulated into the evolution of Japan's globalism thus far? These and similar questions are important in discussions of globalism and resource diplomacy.

Aid and Its Articulation into Globalism

To launch itself into the role of a major player in world politics Japan does not hesitate to use its power economic capabilities to affect events in the changing global system. In January 1990, with all the changes unfolding in Eastern and Central Europe, it decided to play a role in reshaping Europe by announcing an aid package of more than $1 billion in loans and grants for Poland and Hungary. During a ten-day visit to Europe in January 1990, Prime Minister Kaifu announced the aid package as specifically targeted (1) for assistance to Poland and Hungary for the import of machinery and capital goods from Japan and other countries; (2) to encourage the two countries to open up their economies to market forces and to negotiate debt rescheduling; and (3) to convey the willingness of Japanese companies to extend their investments to Eastern Europe if conditions are made conducive and if the liberalization of the economies continued.[2] In making this headstart into the former Communist bloc Japan is expressing its determination to play both an economic as well as a political role in the emerging new Europe. According to Japanese officials, Japan wants to be viewed not merely as an economic actor but as an entity that can help maintain and shape the future world order.

The above pattern of behavior corresponds very well with Japan's newly-acquired dominant creditor status. In 1989 it surpassed the United States to become the world's foremost donor of foreign aid, providing nearly $9 billion in ODA. In yen terms it was a foreign aid increase of 5.6 percent to developing countries.[3] This trend in Japanese economic power is vastly different from its situation in the immediate post World War II period of 1945-1951 when as a defeated nation it was physically occupied by forces under General MacArthur. It regained its sovereignty again in 1952 following the signing of the San Francisco Treaty the previous year. With the political emancipation Japan's immediate foreign policy objectives focused on the pursuit of economic measures as a principal vehicle for global influence. Domestic reconstruction and in particular the development of the Japanese economy became the immediate preoccupation. In international relations the United States became Japan's sponsor in many International Governmental Organization (IGOs) like the International Monetary Fund (IMF), the General Agreements on Tariffs and Trade (GATT), and the United Nations. Many aspects of its international relations were facilitated by United States military cooperation and assistance up till 1973. Japan's almost exclusive reliance on the United States in foreign policy issues gave it more time to develop overseas trade as a key component of its domestic economic recovery. By the late 1950, Japan was already in the process of establishing several trade relationships throughout the world, in addition to having secured the United States market as its main exporting avenue.

The extensive ravages of World War II only served as a precipitating factor in Japan's determined effort to accelerate economic development. The Japanese economic developmental ethos can be traced back to history. With the Meiji Restoration in the late 1860s, the state embraced a pro developmental orientation and proclaimed the goal of "rich country, strong military" (*fukoku kyohei*) as the guiding premise of the new Japanese state.[4] The Meiji Era was significant in terms of Japan's modernization and rise in the global arena. During this period, Emperor Meiji began reforms along Western lines. The main features which set the Meiji Restoration apart as the beginning for a modern Japan can be classified under political and constitutional development, foreign relations, and economic progress. The changes that were introduced were what launched Japan on its rise to global dominance.

Against the background of three hundred years of early modern Japanese history, Emperor Meiji's reign (1867-1912) stands out as a time of deliberate modernization. During the Tokugawa period, certain pre-conditions for modernization had developed. These pre-conditions were of vital importance but were purely accidental because concepts like modernization and progress were never consciously adopted as social and administrative goals. The new official policy of the nation was to reform along Western lines. The people of Japan had divided opinions regarding this foreign influence.[5] A prevailing opinion at Kyoto at the time was in keeping the door tightly shut, in breaking all agreements with the Westerner, and in ousting him and all his ways. But the end of the shogunate marked the beginning of a new age and an end to this prevailing opinion. Japan's government and people in the Meiji era wanted to catch up with the technologically advanced nations of the West. In striving to achieve this goal, they absorbed enough Western civilization to profoundly affect their society at all levels.

Emperor Meiji, as he was known to Westerners, was Japan's first modern emperor and ascended the throne when he was only fourteen. He came to recognize through his advisors that the foreigner must be accepted. The monarch announced his intention to stand by the treaties with the Western nations made by the shogun, and to supervise directly relations with external powers. However, the government and people felt like they had been forced to sign the treaties, and revision should therefore occur since they felt the treaties relegated them to an inferior status. Full revision of the treaties did not occur until the end of the Meiji reign.[6] The Meiji Restoration of 1868, apart from its importance in Japanese history, has proved to be a major event in modern world history. The Emperor's reign was called Meiji which means "enlightened government." From 1868 to 1894, when foreign affairs began to be dominant in the national mind, the chief interest of the nation was to be focused on domestic reorganization. The first need of the state was centralization. The first step toward centralization had been when the shogunate was abolished, but it was only the first step. There was no adequate machinery for carrying on the government under the new regime, because for nearly eight hundred years the emperor had delegated his authority to the Bakufu.

In 1868 the capital was moved from Kyoto to Yedo, which was renamed Tokyo—"Eastern Capital"—and the Emperor took up his residence in the castle-palace of the shogun. No longer was the emperor kept in veiled seclusion. The transfer of the capital brought the emperor nearer to the geographic center of Japan and closer to the foreigners. He even issued an edict denouncing all violence against them. Public clamor for abolishing feudalism began. Civil officials were appointed to represent the central government in each of the fiefs, and a bureaucracy controlled by Tokyo was begun. In 1869 the vast majority of the nearly three hundred feudal lords voluntarily surrendered their fiefs.[7] The love of country nurtured by centuries of union under the Tokugawa and the loyalty developed by Bushido, was newly aroused by contact with Western peoples. This love of country made possible a unified administration under the Emperor. The surrender of the fiefs was followed in 1871 by an imperial edict which finally abolished feudalism.

The end of feudalism was followed in the course of the next few years by acts which perfected as thoroughly a centralized government as the most highly organized states of the West. A national army was substituted for the old feudal army. This army was drawn from all ranks of society. The new army was first patterned after French models, and then after the German system following the Franco-Prussian War. An act closely related to the nationalizing of the military service was the removal of many of the old social distinctions. The difference between the civil or court nobility and the military class was abolished. The new aristocracy that was later created was neither civil nor military, but national. The former distinctions between the warriors and the commoners were canceled. By 1876, all subjects of the Emperor were now on equal footing in the eyes of the law.

In place of the local administration by feudal lords, an elaborate bureaucracy was organized. Its members were appointed by and were responsible to the authorities in Tokyo, and to it was entrusted the entire administration of the country, local as well as national. The bureaucracy was made up largely of members of the samurai class at the beginning because they had been the only ones trained in government administration.[8] However, as time went on, the ranks of the civil service were recruited from the successful candidates at competitive examinations. These exams were open to all classes. The model of this bureaucracy was found partly in the reforms of the seventh and eighth centuries. The Japanese, however, were influenced as well by Western models, the example of Germany being especially strong in subsequent years. The leaders in the reform movement planned a national code of laws. The new government pushed as rapidly as possible for the formation of codes along Western models. By 1871 two volumes of the criminal code were ready. The use of torture and of punishments which, judged by Western standards, are excessive or barbarous, was abolished. Trial by jury was not adopted, but a judicial system was begun and every effort was made to make it efficient.

The currency system was thoroughly reorganized and nationalized. There was always confusion and instability under the feudal system. The newly centralized government was under the necessity of starting a uniform national currency. The support of the mercantile classes would then be assured, and every new coin and bull would be evidence to the people of the power of the Emperor and the Tokyo administration. National prosperity would also be prompted. A commissioner was sent to the U.S. to study its finances. When he returned, the decimal system was introduced, a new coinage was issued, and a plan of national banks and paper currency was adopted which resembled the one in the United States.[9] It was later modified by the foundation of a central national bank along Western lines. The central national bank strengthened the control exercised by its central government over the banking organization of the nation. It also aided in the marketing of government bonds and in the financing of its other undertakings.

Japan turned toward directing an industrial revolution. Economic changes were initiated by the state. The programs were so large and so basic that only the government possessed the funds and the ability to execute plans. There was relatively little capital in private hands. Even if private parties had the funds, they often did not desire to gamble on large-scale undertakings, at least not without official support. In addition to direct official control and operation of key industries, the government did extend considerable aid and subsidies to encourage the development of certain specified private industries. The government did not adhere to any preconceived concepts of state socialism or of dedication to private enterprise but rather used pragmatic means to solve economic problems. They held foreign advisers to a minimum because they feared that foreign assistance might come with political strings attached.

The centralization of the government was not completed without a struggle with the forces of the *ancien regime*. Most of the nation was behind its reform leaders, but every step in advance was met with violent opposition. There was extreme anti-foreign attitudes from those defenders of the old regime. In 1877, the opposition started a well organized rebellion in the South. The suppression of the rebellion had taxed the powers of the new government, but the new national order had met the old on the field of battle and had conclusively demonstrated its superiority. The new national army, drawn from all classes, had overwhelmed the forces of feudalism and serious armed opposition to the new age was at an end.

The triumph of centralization was but one phase of the potential transformation of Japan during the Meiji period. There was a movement towards a constitutional government which had resulted from contact with the West. The systems in Germany and Prussia represented one group's ideal. The British system represented another group's ideal. After an official mission returned from the United States and Europe, a "memorandum monarchy" was presented.[10] This was the true beginning of the struggle for representative government. No one ever talked of abolishing the monarchy because the imperial institution had too firm a hold on the imagination of the nation. The movement for representative government drew its support from the two groups of people. These two factions were reconciled after a compromise was arranged. Important constitutional changes were agreed upon which was a small step toward representative government.

A senate was established as a legislative chamber. It was to have deliberative powers but not those of initiating measures, and it was to be made up exclusively of appointed members of the noble and official classes. There was to be a reorganization of the departments, including the establishment of a high court of justice, to obtain a separation between the judicial, executive, and legislative branches of government. This was obviously done on the lines of the Western model of "The theory of the division of functions." In addition, "an assembly of the governors of the prefectures" was to be convened to bring the Tokyo authorities in touch with the needs of the people.[11] None of these changes provided for popular election or for representation of any but the official classes, but they were meant to limit the absolute power of the group that surrounded the Emperor. Neither the Senate nor the assembly of governors proved very effective because both were easily controlled by the ministry.

By 1877, the desire for a constitution was evident. It was no longer confined to liberal or dissatisfied members of the ruling class. The movement grew in intensity after lectures and agitators instructed and aroused the people. Eventually there were elected bodies which served as advisors to the governors. They served to give the people a voice in local finances and were training schools for the national parliament. In particular, the demands for liberal reforms only increased after these local assemblies were formed. There was call for a national assembly. Finally in October of 1881, the government yielded and in the name of the Emperor promised that a national assembly would be convened in 1890 and that a constitution would be granted. Prince Ito was sent abroad to study the constitutions of the West. When he returned, he became the head of the commission that would draft a similar document.

Following the promise of 1881 for a national assembly, three parties arose to prepare the way for government under a constitution. The three parties were the Liberal Party, the Liberal Conservatives, and the Constitutional Imperialists. Each party had very different ideas about how things in government should operate which caused party agitation. They were still unprepared for the party system operating in a constitution such as that of England. When Ito returned in 1882, preparations to reorganize the government, which involved the adoption of a constitution, began almost immediately. Of all the limited monarchies, he liked Bismarck's Germany the best. He began in 1884 by restoring the nobility. The next step was the remodeling of the cabinet to a form corresponding somewhat to that of Germany. The prime minister, like the German chancellor, was now to have the guidance of all the other ministers, and was to be responsible for the entire conduct of the administration. Official appointments to the civil service were to be based upon their success in examinations which were open to all subjects of the Emperor.

The constitution itself was to be granted by the Emperor out of his own kindness, and in constructing it the nation was to have no direct voice. In 1889, the completed constitution was accepted by the Emperor and was officially proclaimed by him. He was the source of all authority and combined in himself all sovereignty. He sanctioned all laws and ordered them to be proclaimed and executed. He was the head of the executive branch of government. All Japanese were to be liable for taxes and military service, but, subject to the restrictions imposed by law, they had equal rights to appointment to office. They could change their homes, their houses were free from search, and they had freedom of speech, public assembly, writing, association, and religion. These laws, however, were "subject to the restrictions placed by law."

Despite its modern form, the Meiji constitution embraced some traditional aspects of Japanese politics. The ideal state was the patriarchal family headed by the Emperor as father of the nation, government of men prevailed above government by law, group obligations took precedence over individual rights, and man by nature was created unequal. These were all traditional Japanese beliefs.

Of almost equal interest to the development of politics, a constitution, and economic progress, is the development of foreign relations. The establishment of the diplomatic legations of Western powers in Tokyo was allowed and the Emperor on the advice of his ministers received the foreign diplomats in person and tried to maintain friendly relations between them and his administration. Japanese legations were established in the capitals of the various treaty powers, and Japan sought to conform itself to the international ways of the West. Before the Meiji Restoration, Japan had been isolationist in its foreign policy. Although primary concern was with charting domestic affairs, a concurrent military build-up laid the basis for the initial acquisition of territories off the islands surrounding Japan and on the Asian mainland. Japan had turned to overseas expansionism. Although this new philosophy was interrupted by the war and eventual defeat, it gained added momentum during the American occupation and 1950s era of accelerated growth. The main exception is that the "strong military" component of the Meiji philosophy has been deemphasized.

In addition to the contribution of Allied policy which broke the international isolation of the 1940s and the Japanese Meiji economic ethos itself, the remarkable post World War II economic recovery could be attributed to the motivating effects of other factors. These factors, among others were, a crippling inflation that paralyzed the entire society, and the dismantling of the old business elite (the Zaibatsu) one aspect of Allied Policy. These factors were in turn exacerbated by the sudden increase in Japan's population as a result of the repatriation of Japanese domiciled and working abroad, the loss of its empire and the political transformation of China and Southeast Asia, its main trading partners. The above factors also contributed to a critical shortage of capital within the Japanese economy thereby making Japan more dependent on the United States for a substantial portion of its basic needs.

In the midst of all these problems and preoccupation to turn the economic tide around, Japan's ODA had its origins in its postwar reparation activities. In the mid to late 1950s Japan was simultaneously pursuing industrial development, building up export markets, securing access to new low-cost energy and raw materials, and seeking to settle postwar reparations claims. Japan skillfully integrated its industrial objectives, its reparation activities, and its voluntary bilateral ODA programs, such that the last two objectives contributed to the objectives of industrial development. Because of the utmost priority given to national development the *yon shocho* ("four ministries and agency") ended up dominating the decision making process to ensure that the reparations program contributed to certain national economic development goals. In reparations payments Japan fully tied the disbursement of reparations to the procurement of Japanese goods and services.

Developments in the latter part of the 1980s have confirmed the economic ascendancy of Japan as the world's largest creditor nation and the United States as the world's largest debtor nation. The global expectations that come with the role of foremost creditor account for the substantial focus Japan is directing at economic cooperation in general, and more specifically, foreign aid to developing countries. Before elaborating on Japanese foreign policy objectives that foreign aid programs are believed to serve, it is essential to first clarify the concept of foreign aid and also make reference to particular aid programs that are central to the power economic attributes and behavior of Japan in the global system.

Some Conceptual Clarifications

To start with, this examination of Japanese foreign aid focuses on total resource flows which is the flow of funds to developing countries and international facilities. Included in this transfer are grants and long-term capital transactions made by the government and government related entities, private long term capital transactions and donations made by private non-profit and voluntary organizations. Foreign aid itself is a broad category of resource transfer that includes in the case of Japan one key element: Official Development Assistance (ODA). According to Japanese official views, ODA as a component of resource flows to developing countries and international facilities is for the purpose of economic development and welfare needs, with transactions based on easy terms and conditions. ODA therefore has a grant element which is defined as the difference between the face value of the loan and the discounted present value of the amount of amortization and interest payments to be made in the future by the borrowing country. In this sense a grant has by definition, a grant element of 100 percent, while a loan with a higher interest rate and a shorter maturity period has a lower grant element. In 1988 the grant share and the overall grant element of Japan's foreign aid declined to 36.3 percent and 73.2 percent, respectively, from 1987's levels of 47.3 percent and 75.4 percent.[12]

Japanese aid, like aid from other DAC members could also be tied or untied. The untying of aid generally means not to restrict the source of procurement of goods and services made by the aid to the donor nation. Aid can be extended in the form of loans, grants, or technical assistance. Most Japanese aid is denominated in yen. This further means that the Japanese government has to decide whether a yen loan or grant will be tied to a specific project or whether it will be program assistance. The latter finances developing countries' structural adjustment programs. Technical assistance, on the other hand, can involve sending specialists abroad, inviting trainees to Japan, dispatching Japan Overseas Cooperation Volunteers (the counterparts of the American Peace Corps Volunteers), implementing development projects, among others. Contracts for loans and grants related to projects and programs are usually concluded between the governments of the recipient countries and Japanese companies.

Japan's ODA can be broken down into grants and grantlike aid (these include technical assistance and other grants), development lending, and contributions to multilateral institutions. In 1986 Japan's total ODA amounted to $5,634 million with grants and grantlike aid making up $1,703 million, and contribution to multilateral institutions totalling $1,788 million. Technical assistance which falls in the category of grants and grantlike aid accounted for $849 million. The rest comprised of $2,143 million in development lending.[13]

Japan's past aid performance in terms of ratio of aid to GNP, grant element, and level of procurement-tying does not compare favorably with that of most other OECD donors. Between 1982–1987 its ratio of ODA expenditures to GNP was 0.3 percent below the average of the 18 donors of OECDs Development Assistance Committee. In 1987 that placed it 12th among DAC donors. In 1989 at 0.32 percent of GNP it again ranked 12th among the principal donor nations in the 24 member OECD. It was well below Norway (1.02 percent and first place) and

Denmark (1 percent and second place). In the past as well Japan has had the lowest grant share among DAC nations. This means that a substantial portion of its aid comes in the form of concessionary loans. In 1986 for instance the grant share of the top six DAC donors followed this order: United States (91.1 percent); Japan (60.7 percent); France (78.1 percent); West Germany (75.6 percent); Italy (90.2 percent); and the Netherlands (93.7 percent). The following year Japan's grant share was even lower (47.3 percent) and far below the DAC average of 84.3 percent.[14]

Japanese grant funded projects, like those of other donors, are generally procurement-tied. This has resulted in Japanese aid being criticized for giving priority to the corporate concerns of Japanese companies, or simply serving the interest of Japan Inc. A more detailed critique of the Japanese aid program will be presented in later sections of this chapter.

In terms of foreign aid figures and tables in particular a few final distinctions must be made to ensure adequate understanding. First, it is useful to distinguish between foreign aid commitments and foreign aid disbursements. The former refers to obligations to provide aid to recipient nations under specified terms; funds may be committed in one year but not disbursed until later years; the latter refers to the actual transfer of the resources. A second distinction that is essential is that between figures in current dollars (that is figures based on actual price recorded at the time of the aid disbursement), and constant dollars (that is values reflecting prices that prevailed in a single base year). Most of the data sources listed above are based on current dollars only.

Japan's current preoccupation with a more global role has been reflected in part in a recent noticeable increase in the value of Japanese aid outlays expressed in dollars. In terms of performance Japan's ODA flows surpassed the $10 billion level for the first time in Fiscal year 1988. This significant step resulted from the initial implementation of the government's fourth medium-term plan for official development aid. According to the plan the goal is to increase cumulative ODA spending to $50 billion or more over the 1988–1992 five-year period. If this goal is achieved, it would mean doubling the amount of foreign aid distributed over the previous five years (1983–1987). In keeping with the plan also a larger foreign aid package was allocated for the 1989 Fiscal Year (April 1989—March 1990). Figure 3.1 presents the transition of total ODA flows to developing countries from 1979 to 1989. Categories in the transition include both bilateral and multilateral

Figure 3.1   **Trends in the Aggregate Flow
of Japan's ODA: 1980–1990**

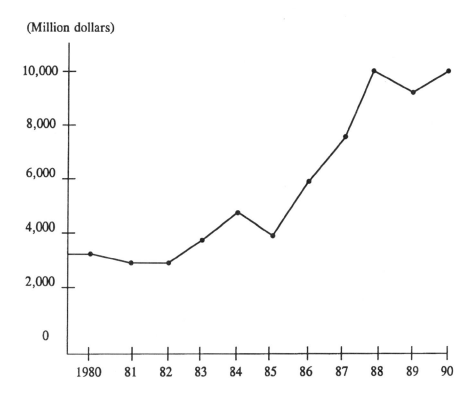

Source: Adapted from *Japan's Official Development Assistance* Annual
Reports.

disbursements in the ODA category, and in other Official Development Finance categories.

Even before the 1980s, Japan's foreign aid program took off in earnest in the 1960s. In the second half of the 1970s the government embarked on a series of medium-term plans to widen the scope of its ODA. The first plan adopted in 1977 aimed at doubling the annual value of aid to $2.8 billion in the 1978–80 period. The plan was a success because the 1980 total reached $3.3 billion. The second plan had as its objective extending aid to the value of $24 billion in the 1981–1985 period. This goal fell short of its target by $6 billion since the actual total was only $18 billion. In September 1985, a third plan was adopted with the aim of providing at least $40 billion in aid during the seven-year period of 1986–1992. However, the sudden appreciation of the yen that began in September 1985 made the objectives of the plan easy to achieve well ahead of time. The yen's appreciation jerked up the dollar value of Japan's ODA.

Prior to the Toronto summit of advanced industrial democracies in June 1988, the fourth medium-term plan, which is referred to above was initiated. As a result, the value of the ODA outlays shot up to $10 billion in Fiscal year 1988 (April 1988 to March 1989).[15] In 1987 Japan's ODA package totalled $7.5 billion. Largely because of the 1988–1992 foreign assistance plan, and the yen's strength, in 1989 Japan's ODA surpassed the nonmilitary foreign aid of the United States to occupy the topmost rank among donors. Japan's commitment to increased foreign aid flows is reflected in the generous appropriations to the aid budget despite government caution on spending in social welfare, public works, and other sectors of the Japanese society. In spite of Japan's remarkable ODA performance expressed in dollars, its past aid performance does not compare favorably with that of most other OECD donors when its aid expenditures is expressed as a ratio of GNP. Table 3.1 shows the trend in aid performance when aid is expressed as a percentage of GNP for the 18 principal DAC countries from 1980–1987. Japan's ratio of ODA expenditures to GNP has been only 0.3 percent, below the average of the 18 DAC countries. Expressed in yen as a percentage of GNP its ODA flows have also been consistently lower compared to other members. This weakness in Japan's foreign aid-giving behavior will be discussed in more detail in later portions of this chapter.

Table 3.1

ODA as Percentage of GNP for 18 DAC Countries: 1980–1987

Country	1980	1981	1982	1983	1984	1985	1986	1987
Australia	0.48	0.41	0.56	0.49	0.45	0.48	0.47	0.33
Austria	0.23	0.33	0.36	0.24	0.28	0.38	0.21	0.17
Belgium	0.50	0.59	0.58	0.59	0.58	0.55	0.48	0.49
Canada	0.43	0.43	0.41	0.45	0.50	0.49	0.48	0.47
Denmark	0.74	0.73	0.77	0.73	0.85	0.80	0.89	0.88
Finland	0.22	0.27	0.29	0.32	0.35	0.40	0.45	0.50
France	0.63	0.73	0.74	0.74	0.77	0.78	0.70	0.74
W. Germany	0.44	0.47	0.48	0.48	0.45	0.47	0.43	0.39
Ireland	0.16	0.16	0.27	0.20	0.22	0.24	0.28	0.20
Italy	0.15	0.19	0.20	0.20	0.28	0.26	0.40	0.35
Japan	0.32	0.28	0.28	0.32	0.34	0.29	0.29	0.31
Netherlands	0.97	1.07	1.07	0.91	1.02	0.91	1.01	0.98
New Zealand	0.33	0.29	0.28	0.25	0.25	0.25	0.30	0.26
Norway	0.85	0.85	1.03	1.10	1.03	1.01	1.17	1.09
Sweden	0.79	0.83	1.02	0.84	0.80	0.86	0.85	0.88
Switzerland	0.24	0.24	0.25	0.31	0.30	0.31	0.30	0.31
U.K.	0.35	0.43	0.37	0.35	0.33	0.33	0.31	0.28
U.S.	0.27	0.19	0.27	0.24	0.24	0.24	0.23	0.20

Source: *Japan's ODA 1988 Annual Report.* p. 38.

Prior to the 1989 budgetary stringency related to considerations of balance of payments and foreign exchange reserves,the absence of a strong domestic constituency for foreign aid contributed largely to the low priority accorded the foreign aid budget. The trend persisted even more because there was no single agency to defend the aid package. Accordingly, in the 1970s in particular, the ratio of Japanese aid to GNP was subject to the ups and downs of the country's balance of payments difficulties as reflected in its erratic and fluctuating pattern. The official articulation of the new realization to increase the role of foreign aid as a vehicle of Japan's economic security came in May 1978. Prime Minister

Takeo Fukuda announced that his government would double ODA in the next three years. As a result, in 1978 development aid increased by 55 percent, 19 percent in 1979, and 16 percent in 1980.[16] However, some of the increase was due to a rising exchange rate for the yen reflected in larger dollar figures since aid is reported in United States dollars. Nonetheless in 1979 Japan became the fourth most important donor among OECD countries exceeding the ODA/GNP ratio of the United States for the first time. Still Japan's ODA/GNP ratio remained below the OECDs DAC average. In response to continued external criticisms the government embarked on a more ambitious aid program in the 1980s.

However, the new resolve to increase the amount of foreign aid was undermined by falling exchange rate for the yen. In 1981, Japanese ODA fell both in absolute terms and as a percentage of GNP. Aid fell by $225 million (6.7 percent) although overall government expenditures increased by over 5.8 percent. The ODA/GNP ratio slipped back to 0.28 percent.[17] While Japan was making the effort to increase its aid package, it was also trying to liberalize the terms on which it was distributing the aid. In terms of the DAC average, Japan lags behind in the areas of average maturity of loans, average interest rate charged on loans, and the grant element as a share of total ODA.

Rationales and Imperatives

The shifting trends, distributional patterns, and inherent problems in the Japanese aid program are better grasped when put in the context of aid distributional rationales as they underlie specific instances of Japanese foreign policy behavior. The distribution of aid is generally predicated on certain beliefs or expectations that specific foreign policy goals will be realized either in the short or in the long run. Specifically, aid-giving is motivated by expectations which lead us to ask questions such as: Does Japan's aid promote Japanese economic security? Does it enhance political and economic stability in the Third World? Or is Japanese global influence strengthened by resource transfers? These are some of the questions we will be attempting to answer indirectly through a discussion of rationales, objectives, and assumptions underlying Japanese foreign aid as a vehicle of its power economic behavior.

Japan's foreign aid philosophy as a member of the DAC of the OECD is predicated directly on the rationales and assumptions of the 1969 Pearson Commission Report on International Development. It promotes the view that aid should be given as a humanitarian gesture. In other words, rich countries should help poor countries out of a feeling of *noblesse oblige* or what has been referred to as *richesse oblige*—genuine moral concern by rich countries for improved socio-economic conditions in poor countries. This Japanese aid philosophy as articulated by officials of the Japan Economic Cooperation Bureau views aid programs as part of a global welfare system whose objective is to assist poor countries until they graduate into the stage where they can do without foreign assistance. This rationale is linked to the goal of promoting economic and social development in the Third World.

In addition to Japanese aid articulation into basic human needs concerns and the promotion of economic development, geopolitical concerns have found their way into the aid program. It is now the view among top aid officials in the Japan International Cooperation Agency (JICA) and the Overseas Economic Cooperation Fund (OECF), that Japan can more effectively promote its own national interests by promoting the interests of other countries–both developing and developed.[18] As now the world's largest creditor and the fact of its growing economic power projection, it is also in the process of relieving part of the security burden on a United States that is relatively in decline and now the world's largest debtor nation. It would not be a surprise if in the future more cooperation between Japanese aid agencies and the United States Agency for International Development (U.S. AID) is worked out with the aim of getting Japan to coordinate its aid efforts more efficiently and pick up more of the slack created by the dwindling United States aid budget since the early 1980s.

A second objective of foreign aid is therefore to strengthen relations between developing countries and Japan. This goal, it is assumed, would directly benefit taxpayers in one way or another because it is Japanese taxpayers' money that is being spent in the process of extending aid. This means according to Japanese officials, aid should be used in places where it will yield longterm benefits and enhance the power economic capabilities of Japan. It further means that Japan's aid distribution has a geopolitical bias underpinned by geographic proximity. Asian countries are of central importance in the attempt to realize the second objective (improve relations with developing countries). China, Indonesia, and Thailand, three recipients of Japanese aid are viewed as an important part of Japan's national interests. China is important for strategic and other reasons.

Indonesia and Thailand are key members of the Association of South-East Asian Nations (ASEAN) and have historically been on good terms with Japan.

When the two broad foreign aid rationales are considered together, the fact stands out that in all official Japanese statements on foreign aid since the 1950s certain themes have been consistently articulated.[19] Economic interest is the cornerstone of Japan's national interest. Resources are transferred with the objective of alleviating the perennial problems of underdevelopment. Foreign aid is a principal vehicle to articulate and enhance the national interest, in particular economic security. The themes that recur are: protection of national interest, in particular economic interest, expansion of Japanese investment abroad, exportation of Japanese technology and managerial know-how, and enhancing Third World development.

Similar to other major donor nations within the OECD, Japan's foreign aid rationales, objectives, and assumptions are well articulated. The main problem, according to critics, lies in the disjointed (disunited) Japanese aid program because it is being administered by several government bodies. The more experienced foreign aid distributors like the United States, Britain, or France, confine the foreign aid program within a central aid agency. In Japan, it is possible to identify over ten ministries with authority over various aspects of Japan's foreign aid program. The formulation of economic cooperation policies is shared by three ministries: Ministry of Finance (MOF), Ministry of Foreign Affairs (MOFA), MITI, and one agency—the Economic Planning Agency (EPA). Figure 3.2 summarizes the key actors involved in the initiation and disbursement of foreign aid.

The respective aid disbursing government organs hold different views on what purpose aid should serve. In the Ministry of Foreign Affairs, the view is that aid should serve three functions: humanitarian, interdependence of nations, and strategic (Japan's security). MITI views aid in terms of Japan's current role as the world's largest creditor nation. This view is based on the argument that a creditor's responsibility includes expanding overseas investments which is related to the recycling of surplus funds, and the increase of ODA expenditures. The lack of a coherent and unified aid philosophy is again, a reflection of the decentralized nature of ODA administration in Japan. Since the aid program tends to be the main preserve of the four ministries, aid policies are hardly ever debated in the Diet. Ministries promote their own aid philosophies without regard to those of

**Figure 3.2 Japan's ODA: Administration
and Type of Aid**

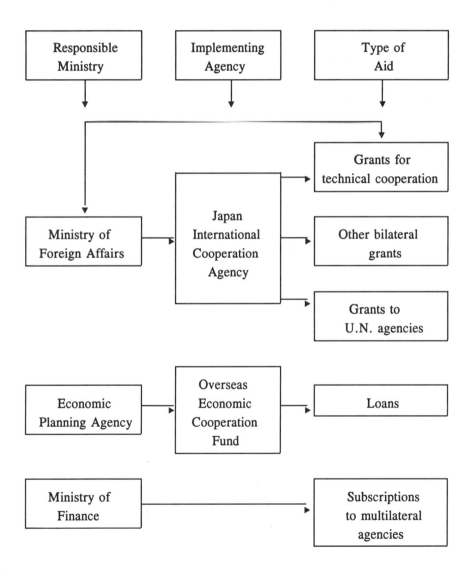

others.   The pursuit of differing objectives at times results in less meaningful struggles over how the aid budget is to be apportioned.   While MITI gives priority to the promotion of the private sector's corporate concerns, the Foreign Ministry focuses on diplomatic considerations and the improvement of Japan's image abroad.   It is very aware of the recipients' concerns over the nature of aid.[20] From the perspective of the recipient, for resource transfer to qualify as aid-granting it must not be stingy.   Untying of the numerous strings attached to aid is often advocated, although critics hold the view that excessive untying might encourage the recipient government to spend the money in areas totally unrelated to what it was intended to do.   The example is often quoted of the Philippines where President Marcos often used Japanese aid to profit his close supporters.   In addition, critics have often pointed to the evaluative inadequacy of completed projects and the charge that assistance often does not reach the poor for whom it is primarily intended.   The consequence is Japanese ODA tends to contribute to the ever widening gap between rich and poor.

Related to the welter of problems is the ongoing change in attitude toward Japan's aid flows.   There has been a recent surge of proposals calling for the reform of current aid disbursement methods and procedures.   The stream of criticisms and proposals is due largely to the fact that Japan now occupies the top place in the distribution of nonmilitary assistance.   More efficient disbursement, implementation, and evaluation, it is assumed, is bound to affect in a positive manner Third World development and poverty.   In response to the expanding role of foreign aid and the increasing interest in the program, in 1988 Prime Minister Noboru Takeshita pledged to make development assistance one of Japan's key tasks.   The Foreign Ministry and the Ministry of Education are together in the process of trying to put together a plan to establish an "international development university," with the objective of making the program more efficient.

The response of aid officials to this criticism of disunity in the aid program is that the variety of ministries and agencies makes it possible to employ their resources, expertise and participation in the implementation of programs and projects.   Critics further point to the fact that the Japanese have little experience and no fixed philosophical bearings to guide their aid program.   Even though foreign aid has become the object of a broad national consensus, there has yet to emerge a clear well-articulated rationale for the conduct of the aid, even within the government.

Most Japanese endorse the aid program as a way for the country to pull its weight in the international community without taking on a more military role. But the general consensus that Japan still lacks a coherent aid philosophy would lead critics to conclude that Japan is stepping up its aid outlays only because of external pressures. The counter response by Japanese aid officials to such a charge is that Japan is dedicated to giving aid because it can no longer afford to live in splendid isolation from international society. Aid-giving in this context is viewed as a vehicle for guaranteeing a peaceful, stable, and better society to the younger generation of Japanese.

The above criticisms of the Japanese aid program constitute what may be called 'soft' and general criticisms. Far stronger criticisms of the program have been made by both Japanese and non-Japanese observers.[21] The first of these criticisms is that despite official statements to the contrary, the Japanese aid philosophy is not motivated by a genuine desire to contribute to global prosperity. Aid is seen as the entrance fee for rich-nation status, or the admission price for the club of rich nations. The evidence cited for this criticism is the low level of Japan's ODA as a percentage of GNP, especially prior to 1989. The 0.32 percent, 0.34 percent, 0.29 percent, and again 0.29 percent ratios for the years 1983–1986 constitute some of the highest ratios for Japan and they are well below the target set by the international community.

The second of these scathing criticism of Japanese foreign aid points to the predominance of Japanese firms in the foreign aid distribution process. To critics the Japanese aid program is primarily a government tool for export promotion. The willingness of Japan to extend development assistance as a humanitarian gesture is strongly questioned. For some aid distribution is merely a way of fulfilling expectations others have of Japan as currently the largest creditor nation in the world, and a member of the club of rich advanced industrial nations. This argument is supported by the fact that the Japanese aid program neglects technical assistance which is one of the most important components of ODA. Besides, technical assistance is germane to LDC development because it covers such activities as conducting surveys and research, and personnel training. The training of local manpower in technical assistance, the critics point out, is especially relevant in projects that involve the drawing up of plans for irrigation schemes, and employing new methods for agricultural development, and improving water supply and sewage systems. Technical assistance is allotted one of the lowest levels of funding among the various aid categories. In 1985 and 1986, for example, development lending was allocated $1,372 and $2,143 million respectively, whereas technical assistance received only $549 and $849 million. In 1987 funding for technical assistance was only $740 million.[22]

The most plausible reason critics cite for Japan's de-emphasis on technical assistance, despite the enormous contribution it can make to LDC development, is that it is not commercially attractive. Technical assistance unlike financial assistance does not involve large sums. In technical assistance much of the expenditure goes to pay technicians, whereas in financial aid involving cooperation to build roads and dams the contracts involved are often lucrative and most of the aid goes toward materials and machinery. These projects usually require only a small number of specialists in relation to their size. Financial aid, because of the large sums involved, is usually a government priority because the government is primarily concerned about the ratio of aid to GNP. The use of assistance as a trade and investment enhancing vehicle for Japanese companies translates into projects being selected more for their relevance and profitability to Japanese companies than for their benefit to the developmental goals of the recipient country.

The gap between theory and practice in Japan's aid-giving, including the importance of the Japanese corporate sector in the entire process, is revealed in the initiation of the assistance process. The process of project identification and recommendation are considered the functions of the recipient nation. The underlying rationale for this policy is two-fold: to prevent Japanese government interference in the internal affairs of a recipient; and to lay the future foundation for the gradual shift of project management to the recipient by ensuring that each project has the full support of the recipient government.[23] In reality, however, project identification is actually carried out by Japanese consulting firms, trading houses, construction companies, and manufacturers. The projects identified by the various elements of the private sector generally fall into the priority category in Japan's foreign aid program. The final contracts are usually won by the companies involved in the initial stages of the aid-giving process. In some cases involving yen financed projects, the recipient nation is in theory free to select a firm from a third country to implement the project. The practice, however, is that Japanese firms have the upper hand since they have often entrenched their influence from the initial stage of project identification, and recommendation, and have inside knowledge about the entire process.

The varied and sometimes conflicting aid-giving rationales are often cited by critics of the program to support their attack on the entire process. In 1987 the Economic Cooperation Bureau's report played into the hands of critics when one of its subtitles read: "Japanese Aid to Meet the Expectations of the World Community."[24] The text below this subtitle elaborated on the theme that Japan must develop its aid program to meet the growing expectations of the world community regarding Japanese aid. As interpreted by critics Japan is engaging in an expanded aid program not of its own free will and on its own initiative, but to accommodate the demands of the global community. To further substantiate this charge critics point to the ambivalence and reluctance in Japanese aid-giving behavior as reflected in its foreign aid record in the 1970s in particular. Prior to its economic superpower status, Japan resisted the idea of the DAC binding members to specific aid commitments. Its reluctance in aid-giving was defended on the grounds that it did not have a colonial experience and so is not obligated to promote development in LDCs. Now with the apparent economic hegemonic decline of the United States, and the corresponding Japanese unmatched record of economic growth, Japanese arguments of balance of payments difficulties, and budgetary deficits are no longer plausible. Moreover, the fast changing regional economic landscape in the United States and Western Europe, has given Japan the realization that it could use its economic prowess, and in particular its foreign aid to enhance its economic security in trade and investment issues on a global scale.

Although Japan lacks cultural experience vis-a-vis a large part of the Third World, in terms of aid diversification versus aid concentration, it compares very favorably with the United States, Britain, and France. The argument can be made that in the years prior to 1988 the Western countries did not significantly outstrip Japan in terms of aid as a percentage of GNP, because most of their aid was geographically concentrated. In 1985, one-third of the United States ODA budget went to Israel and Egypt, resulting in the fact that United States development assistance amounted to only 0.15 percent of GNP out of a total of 0.23 percent compared to Japan's 0.29 percent which was not overly concentrated. One-third of Britain's 0.32 percent of aid as a percentage of GNP went to maintain the *liaison culturelle* between it and its former colonies within the Commonwealth family of nations. In actual fact the British ODA program amounted to only 0.20

percent of GNP in 1985. The French are even more guilty of highly concentrating their aid when viewed in the context of the former colonial relationship and existing overseas territories (*territoires d'Outre Mer*). The French overseas territories are an integral part of France and in 1985 received 0.22 percent and the former colonies 0.23 percent of aid as a percentage of GNP. Unlike Japan, the United States, Britain, and France heavily concentrate their aid because aid is primarily a vehicle used to promote special relationships and enhance strategic objectives.

Summary

In the immediate post-World War II period, the Asian region was the recipient of virtually all Japanese foreign assistance. In this present era of deconcentration of hegemony, Japan's foreign aid program is undergoing rapid geographic diversification to include Africa and Latin America. The push for diversification is being particularly created by the trend toward regional economic blocs as well as the increasing pervasiveness of Japanese multinationals doing business in Africa, Latin America, and the Middle East. Besides, the global expectations that come with the status of foremost creditor nation account for the substantial focus that Japan is directing at economic cooperation in general, and more specifically foreign aid to developing countries.

The complementary role of Japanese foreign aid to United States regional objectives is an element of mutual power-dependence between the two nations because: (1) Japan and the United States have compatible regional interests, for example, in Central America (Panama and Nicaragua in particular); (2) the compatibility or congruence of interests is structured by commonly perceived threats to their national security; and (3) a perception of mutual dependence bolsters the feeling of *esprit de corps* between the two nations thereby resulting in a greater willingness to engage in burdensharing, enhance bonds of partnership, and in the future lead to a strong relationship of power sharing in a world undergoing a deconcentration of hegemony. In other words, Japan's aid flows to developing regions may be performing a dual function: an instrument for commercial penetration and a vehicle to realize United States foreign policy objectives.

Japanese policy pronouncements—the Fukuda Doctrine, economic security, comprehensive national security, among others—have played a very central role in the conduct of Japanese foreign aid policy because they constitute: (1) a justification for the extension of foreign aid; (2) a strategy for expanding foreign aid's articulation into the conduct of foreign policy; and (3) a basis for the conduct of an effective foreign economic policy. Japan's foreign policy is characterized by a proclivity to react to foreign economic threats through policy pronouncements. This trend has been particularly more pronounced since the 1973–74 oil crisis. The natural proclivity for policy pronouncements could be interpreted as a case of economic superpower confidence that is manifested in the need to project domestic values to other parts of the world. Moreover, as an economic superpower, Japan now realizes that it has global interests but at the same time it also has a global responsibility to ensure peace, and an obligation to help peaceful and friendly states. Furthermore, the complementary character of Japan's foreign aid vis-a-vis the shrinking United States economic aid package helps to maintain the liberal international economic status quo.

70 *Chapter 3*

Endnotes

1 For further details on Japan's power economic capabilities, see *Japan's Official Development Assistance 1988 Annual Report* (Tokyo: Ministry of Foreign Affairs, 1989) pp. 3–4; R. Taggart Murphy, "Power Without Purpose: The Crisis of Japan's Global Financial Dominance," *Harvard Business Review*, March—April 1989, pp.72–74; and George Thomas Kurian, *Facts on File National Profiles: Japan* (New York: Facts on File Inc., 1990).

2 See, for example, *JEI Report*, No. 42B (by Barbara Wanner), November 3, 1989, pp. 4–7.

3 For details on the role of ODA in promoting international cooperation, see discussions of the Maekawa Report, *JEI Report*, No. 39A, October 14, 1988.

4 For works on the historical and post-World War II aspects of Japan's economy, see, G.C. Allen, *A Short Economic History of Modern Japan* (New York: Praeger, 1962); Ardath Burks, *Japan: Profile of a Post industrial Power* (Boulder: Westview, 1984); T.J. Pempel, *Policy and Politics in Japan: Creative Conservatism* (Philadelphia: Temple University Press, 1982); and Edwin O. Reischauer, *Japan: The Story of a Nation* (New York: Alfred Knopf, 1974).

5 For further details, see R.H.P. Mason, and J.G. Caiger, *A History of Japan* (New York: The Free Press, 1972).

6 See, for example, Noel F. Busch, *The Horizon Concise History of Japan* (New York: American Heritage Publishing Co., 1972).

7 For further details, see R.H.P. Mason, and J.G. Caiger, *A History of Japan.*

8 See, for example, Kenneth Latourette, *The History of Japan* (New York: The MacMillan Co., 1957); and Upton Close, *Behind the Face of Japan* (New York: Appleton-Century Co., 1942).

9 See, R.H.P. Mason, and J.G. Caiger, *A History of Japan.*

10 For further details, see Milton W. Meyer, *Japan A Concise History* (Boston: Allyn and Bacon, Inc., 1966).

11 See, for example, R.H.P. Mason, and J.G. Caiger, *A History of Japan*; and Donand H. Shively, *Tradition and Modernization in Japanese Culture* (Princeton: Princeton University Press, 1971).

12 *JEI Report*, No. 41A, (by Gretchen Green) October 27, 1989, p.11.

13 *JEI Report*, No. 41A, Oct. 27, 1989, p. 3.

14 "Display: Japan's ODA Performance," *Economic Eye A Quarterly Digest of Views from Japan*, Vol. 10, No. 1. (Keiza, Koho Center, Japan Institute for Social and Economic Affairs, Spring 1989) p. 15.

15 For a summary discussion of the various aid plans, see for example, "Focus on Foreign Aid," *Japan Echo*, Vol. XVI, No. 7, Spring 1989, pp. 6–7.

16 For further details on the stages of Japan's aid policy, see William L. Brooks and Robert M. Orr, Jr., "Japan's Foreign Economic Assistance," *Asian Survey*, XXV, No. 3, (March 1985); Alan Rix, *Japan's Aid Program*, International Development Issues, No.1, (Australian Government Publishing Service, 1987); and Ardath W. Burks, *Japan: A Post Industrial Power* (Boulder: Westview Press, 1990).

17 *Japans ODA, 1988 Annual Report* (Tokyo: Ministry of Foreign Affairs, 1989) p. 38.

18 For the competing views among Japanese aid officials on the role of Japan's foreign aid, see, "Shortcomings of the Foreign Aid Program," *Economic Eye*, Vol. 10, No. 1, Spring 1989, pp.16–19.

19 See for example, opposing views of Japan's Foreign Aid, in *Japan Echo* Vol. XVI, No. 1, Spring 1989, pp.8–12; 19–22.

20 For a more current and balanced analysis of various aspects of Japan's foreign aid program, see, *Shafigul* Islam (ed.) *Yen For Development: Japanese Foreign Aid and the Politics of Burden-Sharing* (New York: Council on Foreign Relations Press, 1991).

21 On criticism of Japan's foreign aid program, see, Abe Motoo, "Foreign Aid: A Dissenter's View," *Japan Echo* Vol. XVI, No. 1, Spring 1989, pp. 19–22; and *JEI Report*, No. 41A (by Gretchen Green), October 27, 1989.

22 *Japan's ODA, 1988 Annual Report* (Tokyo, Ministry of Foreign Affairs, 1989) p. 40; and Sunday O. Agbi, *Japan's Attitudes and Policies Towards African Issues Since 1945: A Historical Perspective* (Tokyo: Institute of Developing Economies, 1982) V.R.F. Series No. 96.

23 See, for example, Interview by Koichiro Matsuura, "Administering Foreign Aid: The View from the Top," *Economic Eye*, Vol. 10, No. 1, Spring 1989, pp. 12–14.

24 Fore more details, see, "ODA wa senskinkoku Kurabu no sankahi de wa nai," in *Economics Today*, Summer 1988, pp. 88–97.

4

INTERDEPENDENCE OF TECHNOLOGY

Technology is the foundation of economic power. It constitutes the pinions on which the overall capabilities of the advanced industrial countries are supported. In particular, it has structured and defined the character of United States hegemonic leadership and is currently the engine of Japan's economic globalism. Hence, changes in the technological balance between the United States and Japan is bound to have far-reaching bilateral and global ramifications. In this chapter, we intend to examine the structural, procedural, and substantive turbulence underlying the United States-Japan technological relationship. In the process instances of cooperation and conflict between the two nations will be identified as they relate to changes in their relative economic power. The analysis is predicated on specific recurrent themes in the technological relationship between the two nations. For example, growing parity in scientific and technological capabilities between the two countries is bound to create tensions and affect the pace and level of cooperation between them. Second, technological innovation as an aspect of economic development is affected by the role of government in the economy. For some countries government intervention in the economy seems to be strongly correlated with growth in scientific and economic capabilities. Two aspects of government intervention can be identified: first is government support for industrial and research policies in the form of funding for Research and Development (R&D); second is the extent of government interference with the market which is manifested specifically in the form of protectionism—for example making it difficult to obtain licensing patents.

United States-Japan Technological Development

In less than fifty years after World War II, Japan has transformed its economy from an exporter of inexpensive toys to the world's key source of sophisticated consumer and industrial products. As now the world's second largest economic entity in the Western industrial world, it is taking traditional markets away from the United States and Western Europe, a manifestation that its industrial technology has equalled and in some instances surpassed that of other industrialized countries in sophistication. Stated differently, its current economic preeminence is in fact reflected in its scientific and technological accomplishment—having progressed from a level of incipient scientific infrastructure to international technological sophistication.[1] Related to this outcome is the fact that a number of U.S. high technology industries have already slipped behind foreign competitors like Japan and the U.S. position of global leader in both science and its industrial applications is encountering formidable challenge.

Japan's technological potential was evident way back in the Meiji period when the country transformed itself into an industrial power, and by World War II Japan was capable of producing complex weapons such as the Zero fighter aircraft. In the post World War II period and the 1960s in particular, Japan moved so effectively into high technology products that it occupied number two position in the technology competition in the 1980s. In its early post World War II years of technological development Japan began by importing existing technology and required natural resources mostly from the United States and has always been particularly adept at commercial applications of scientific discoveries.

After a short period of technology transfer from external sources and the modernization of industries, by the late 1950s greater emphasis was placed on efforts to promote Japan's own science and technology. Accordingly, the Science and Technology Agency was established in 1956, and in 1959 the Council for Science and Technology was organized as an advisory body to the prime minister.[2] Based on the recommendations of the Council, the government outlined in 1986 the General Guidelines for Science and Technology Policy up to the early 1990s. The basic guidelines encompassed three objectives: (1) promote basic research and strengthen original science and technology; (2) specific emphasis on international contributions of science and technology; and (3) promote an interactive harmony between science and technology and human society.

Although in the United States-Japan technological relationship Japan is perceived as the great imitator and the U.S. as the innovator, nonetheless Japan has made tremendous technological strides and avoided the trap of dependent development largely because it has avoided the technological quagmire of licensing dependency, a condition which has been described this way:

> A strategy of relying heavily on licensing innovations by others is likely to be self-defeating, rather than economically-wise: (1) because licenses rarely catch up with innovations within technologies involved—thus tending to ensure continued lags; and (2) because failure to keep close to the current frontiers of technology undermines not only the prospects of catching up with competitors, but also undermines a firm's ability to make prompt and effective use of the licensed technologies.[3]

Japan has escaped the condition of a technological colony and has enhanced its international technological competitiveness basically because of its vigorous research programs aimed at also achieving competitive advantage through development of innovations.

The United States technological leadership which emerged at the close of World War II has, of course, been an integral part of American hegemonic leadership and of Japan's own technological evolution. The end of World War II transformed the U.S. economy and along with it its technological capabilities stretched by wartime production process. Europe and Japan, on the other hand, were ravaged and prostrate economies. In addition to capabilities acquired prior to and during the war, the scope of the American educational process was also an important factor. Second, during the 1950s, the United States for the first time involved the government in the provision of extensive funding for university research. But by the beginning of World War II, the American system of university scientific research had already achieved a respectable status, although not superior to that of Europe.[4] The launching of government university research support through the programs of the National Science Foundation and the National Institutes of Health contributed in large measure in later years to the United States' lead in most fields of technological expertise. In the 1950s and 1960s and still today foreign students, including Japanese students flock to U.S. universities to learn science. The third reason for the United States technological lead was the establishment of a massive system to support military industrial research as part of the military-strategic-defensive objectives of the U.S. Department of Defense (DOD) and later the National Aeronautics and Space Administration (NASA).

During the 1950s and on to the 1960s about half of the total industrial R&D expenditure could be accounted for by the DOD and NASA. The leading edge technologies of the 1950s and 1960s—computer and semiconductor technologies—were an area of clear American technological dominance.[5] Dominance in this area was due largely to military R&D support.

With postwar recovery of Europe and Japan the United States leadership role was bound to face increasing competition—that is the inevitability of U.S. decline is related to the economic recovery of Europe and Japan. However, a challenge to the inevitability-of-the-relative-decline argument is the fact that the U.S. decline continued into the 1980s and the 1990s have not experienced any significant reversal.

Japan, Western Europe and other competitors, although proud of their technological gains are nonetheless uneasy about the eroding preeminence of the United States in most areas. The growing erosion of American technological leadership therefore calls into question a number of factors: (1) its ability to sustain its leadership role in international institutions; (2) the stability of its relationship with increasingly competitive nations; and (3) the wider implications for international stability in economic and military issues of eroding U.S. hegemony. In other words, in high technology industries, world ranking makes an important difference. For the United States slipping from first to second position means a fundamental dramatic shift in the world's strategic balance. For Japan and Western Europe, the challenge to U.S. global preeminence in high technology production implies a challenge to U.S. global hegemony as well as to long-standing commercial interests. The important changes in the economic relationship between the U.S. and Japan as a major trading partner brought about by the decline in U.S. technological preeminence is the focus of the next section of this analysis.

Cooperation and Conflicts

Since the mid 1960s the United States technological balance vis-a-vis Britain, France, West Germany and Japan has been moving towards parity. The most noticeable manifestation of convergence has been in the productivity and income areas.[6] While U.S. productivity grew at a substantial rate during the 1950s and 1960s, European productivity grew at an unprecedented rate, while the rate of growth in Japan was even higher. What are the factors underlying the economic and technological parity? First, with the European and Japanese recovery from the damages of the war, the U.S. advantages had to erode even though U.S. economic and technological leadership was not solely dependent on World War II preparations. According to Nelson, the U.S. had maintained significantly higher productivity levels than Europe and Japan for at least fifty years.[7] Investment in technology and policy decisions in the U.S. led to the domination of high technology industry by the United States. The recovery of Europe and Japan coupled with other factors has contributed to virtually closing the technological gap. First, is the unhindered flow of international trade which has reduced the advantages U.S. firms used to have over access to the world's largest market. Second, the internationalization of technology which has been enhanced by the internationalization of business resulting from the increasing openness of the world economies. Third, other industrialized nations have diverted more funds to research in science and technology and have increased their population trained in science and domestic engineering. The outcome is a greater internal capacity to create new technology and adapt foreign technology to domestic needs. The fourth primary reason behind the convergence was a substantial decline in the spillover from military R&D into civilian technology. Related to the decline is the fact that by 1980 a number of nations had surpassed the U.S. in expenditure on non-military R&D as a percentage of GNP.

During the 1950s and 1960s United States dominance in the area of military technology conferred on the United States significant civilian technological advantages. At present, the dominance in military technology is not spilling over into civilian technology that relates to productivity in the manufacturing industry. The reverse trend instead has been occurring since the late 1960s, spillover has been occurring mainly from civilian to military applications. The frontiers of research in semiconductor and computer technology has focused largely on civilian applications. The U.S. military technological dominance has not helped the U.S. to maintain its overall technological lead, or affect economic growth and competitiveness in favor of the United States.

The United States-Japan technological relationship started with the U.S. primarily licensing technology to Japan.[8] Now, the relationship has been transformed to a level at which the two countries make tremendous research and development contributions to each other and to the world. Japan's approach focuses on technology with both civilian and military applications, a focus that is enormously beneficial to the United States in terms of technological advances in military hardware and high military jets. In fact many experts are of the view that the spectacular triumph of American technology in the Gulf War was also a triumph of Japanese high technology. Japan supplies many key components of America's fighters ranging from the F-15, F-16, and F-18 to the M-1 tank. These weapons could literally not be manufactured without Japanese components. For example, the F-16 fighter pilots would hardly hit their target without Japanese components of the plane's radar. In fact, Japanese machine tools are so vital to America's weapons systems that many American officials are afraid the Japanese would end up controlling America's military destiny. For example, the key components for the computer chips used in the Tomahawk Cruise Missile are controlled by the Japanese. Of twenty-two technologies vital to America's military security, the U.S. leads in only ten. In other words, the memory chips and laser beams that are the core of America's weapons systems are controlled by the Japanese, a reflection of Japan's preeminent position in consumer electronics with military applications.

According to Justin Bloom, Japan's substantial investment in U.S. government R&D projects, is due to three reasons: (1) to gain access to the advanced technology involved; (2) to compensate the U.S. for technical benefits received in the past; and (3) to maintain the relationship in anticipation of future benefits.[9] However, the United States-Japan technology relationship is characterized by both suspicion and trust, cooperation and conflict. Trust and cooperation are reflected in the U.S. invitation to Japan to participate in the U.S. Strategic Defensive Initiative (SDI) project. In contrast, the DOD has also been active in trying to reduce the flow of U.S. scientific and technical information to Japan and other countries. Department of Defense officials went as far as trying to persuade universities to restrict participation of foreign students in unclassified high technology curricula and research projects.

The duality (positive cooperation and "adversarial" cooperation)[10] of the United States-Japan technological relationship is made possible by the scope of cooperation which encompasses both applied and basic technological research. The United States-Japan Advisory Commission in its September 1984 report emphasized this aspect of cooperation when it said:

> The scope and depth of (current) scientific and technological cooperation between
> the United States and Japan is unique. Hundreds of cooperative arrangements
> exist among private corporations; some thirteen government-to-government

agreements are designed to meet public needs; and countless additional inter-changes occur among individual scientists in private and international forums.[11]

Mutual interests and expansiveness of technology are two imperatives that underlie positive cooperation between the two countries. Conflicts between the two countries arise in part from the perception, often correct, that Japan is merely good at exploiting foreign technology, especially from the U.S., without making much effort to establish its own technological base. A second source of conflict centers around the fact that the U.S. strong focus on basic research has not been translated into increased global competitiveness, thereby generating strong U.S. reactions to Japan's success at exploitation and application of technology through highly efficient manufacturing and marketing.

Gerald Dineen in his analysis of the U.S.-Japan science and technology relationship referred to one movement in each country designed to change the current competitive technology relationship.[12] In Japan there is a shift away from the exploitation of foreign technology and an emphasis on funding of basic research. In the U.S., according to Dineen, the movement is still plagued by oscillation: undecided whether it would be beneficial to exploit foreign technology, but at the same time investing in basic research with the aim of regaining its previous competitiveness. The conflicts and differences arise because the two countries have different approaches to the role technology should serve in their national objectives. The U.S. underscores space technology and defense, generally areas of high technology. The Japanese, on the other hand, think along a more basic civilian-oriented marketing level. Their focus is on everyday needs: electronics, automotive, and the like. This difference in investment focus is manifested in the fact that the U.S. surpasses Japan by far in various military technologies (aerospace, jet aircraft, avionics, security-related information processing and so on). Japan does better in technologies with both military and civilian applications thus capturing a large part of the commercial market because of their dual-purpose nature.

The competitive technological relationship notwithstanding, the United States and Japan maintain an extensive network of agreements covering cooperation in virtually every aspect of science and technology. Both governments have made heavy investments in the other's R&D programs, actions motivated largely by political reasons, and second by the flow of useful information between the two countries. The shift from Japanese technological dependence on the U.S. to one of U.S.-Japan technological parity has particularly strengthened the mutual flow of useful information and reinforced the existing elaborate network of agreements on science and technology.   There are increasing instances of the growing interdependence of Japan and the U.S. in joint licensing agreements and joint venture arrangements despite the reference by some observers to a "clash of the titans" in the competitive U.S.-Japan technological relationship. As indicated by the various U.S.-Japan bilateral agreements patterns of cooperation underlie the technological relationship. Cooperative efforts were begun by Japan following World War II when Japan had to draw all its basic research from foreign sources. Domestically, government, industry, and academia pulled their efforts together for development. Despite its recovery and technological sophistication, Japan still considers international participation (especially with the United States) necessary to maintain its competitive advantage.

Currently, a significant amount of Japanese technology is created internally and is transferred to the U.S. either in the form of products or as software through patents and other intellectual property channels. According to the 1984 report of the Science and Technology Agency, Japan exported 241 billion yen worth of technology between April 1982 and March 31, 1983, and imported 279 billion yen worth of technology during the same period. The exports were up 30 percent from the previous year and imports down 1.2 percent from the previous year.[13] The value of technology exported has been on the increase since 1983. The apparent deficit in technology trade is due mostly to contracts still in force that were signed many years back.

Issues impeding the flow of technology between the two countries, according to Martha Harris, are:

(1) Different approaches to protecting innovation; (2) an imbalance in flows of technical information and personnel between the two countries; (3) difficulties in evaluating long-term costs and benefits of bilateral science and technology cooperation; (4) sensitive issues surrounding military technology cooperation; (5) competition between the United States and Japan for sales of technology and products in LDC [less-developed country] markets; (6) structural barriers impeding foreign access to Japanese technology; (7) differences in government resources devoted to formulating and implementing technology transfer policies.[14]

Part of the above impediments have been expressed by some U.S. government, business and academic leaders as an imbalance in favor of Japan in the flow of scientific and technical information, or intellectual property between the two countries. These critics charge that Japan has been a consistent "free-rider" at the expense of the United States, made possible by the United States inclination to publish technical results in detail and to license technology at an extremely low price. In security terms, some argue that U.S. national security could be endangered because hostile countries can more easily obtain illicit advanced technology from Japan than from other sources.

Japan, in other words, is viewed as essentially a competitor and so critics advocate ways by which the U.S. may regain its competitive advantage over Japan in Science and Technology, and others propose a Fortress America approach. In sum, those who advocate such extreme views about the technology imbalance propose that the barriers to achieving greater equity in technology transfers need to be addressed and reduced since the transfer of technology to Japan from the United States is not equal to the flow from Japan to the United States.

The view of the United States-Japan technological relationship in purely adversarial terms is, of course, related to the trading relationship of the two countries.[15] The basic technology from the United States to Japan had significant impact in the areas of computers and communications. Over the years Japan has achieved spectacular commercial success through the quick and effective application of technologies first developed in the United States: The laser (1958); fiber transmission systems (1970); electronic switching (1960); Satellite Transmission (1962); and the mobile cellular radio telephone. The Japanese adaptive technological reflex has contributed in large measure to the U.S.-Japan trade imbalance such that in 1986, the United States trade deficit with Japan was running at an annual rate of $72 billion according to the U.S. Department of Commerce. The imbalance had started in basic industries such as the steel industry, but it has now widened to embrace the high technology areas which have been the stronghold of the United States.

Nineteen Eighty emerged as a turning point for U.S. performance in high technology trade. The surplus earned in previous years in high technology diminished in each subsequent year, reaching a low of $3.6 billion by 1985. In other manufacturing industries the fall was even more significant, where by 1985 they had experienced an enormous deficit of $111 billion. The overall trend has been a deterioration of U.S. performance in most productive categories and in most key trading relationships. The U.S. share of world manufactured exports fell from over 17 percent in 1966 to less than 14 percent by 1983.[16] However, U.S. multinationals maintained their lead with gains in exports of majority-owned foreign subsidiaries making up for the drop in exports from parent firms. In other words, it is foreign affiliates of United States companies that are taking away shares of the world market from U.S. parent companies. The parent companies are not losing their competitiveness to foreign competitors. Thus, based on the above facts, it is not accurate to make reference to a trend of declining U.S. competitiveness.[17] Specifically, discussions that focus on shortcomings of U.S. management innovation are inconsistent with the current market shares of U.S. corporations. The reality is that production activities are experiencing a shift from the United States to foreign locations presumably because of differences in production costs.

Research and Development are also an integral part of the positive and adversarial aspects of the U.S.-Japan science and technology relationship. First, in R&D systems the two countries differ markedly. Much less is spent by the Japanese government to underwrite industrial R&D than in the United States. In 1983, for example, the U.S. government funded 29.3 percent of all business R&D expenditures, whereas the Japanese government supplied barely 1.8 percent.[18] In the United States there has been a move away from U.S. government funding of aircraft, missiles, and telecommunication equipment, to more funding in the iron and steel industry and nonferrous metals. Some Japanese think that because their government underwrites so little of their business sector's R&D in comparison to the U.S. government, the Americans will continue to maintain their advantage in competing with the United States in high technology industries.

The nature of Japan's R&D is closely related to its low-level of defense-related procurement. First, industrial policy in Japan has not been successful at promoting the growth of high technology products. Second, in the areas of trade and industry supply-related incentives predominate over the demand-pull measures. This is manifested in the fact that basic innovative research has been deemphasized in favor of applied research and development. With little government demand for new products and also little support from the government, Japanese firms have focused on commercially feasible paths to R&D. Thus, the Japanese are not known for creating new product designs or whole new industries. Similarly, commercially oriented research as opposed to highly specialized research for military and space applications is still the focus of Japanese engineers and scientists.

In discussions of R&D critics are quick to point out that the U.S. lagged behind in spending relative both to its past spending level and to other advanced industrial nations. This conclusion is based largely on comparisons of R&D expenditure as a percentage of GNP, a measure that shows other nations equal to or even out-spending the United States. Yet in absolute amounts the U.S. expenditure still greatly surpasses any other OECD member, a reflection of the economic size of the nation.

Issues of Technonationalism

The United States plays the most active role in evaluating the science and technology relationship with Japan. Periodic reviews of this relationship are sponsored by the U.S. to determine its usefulness, redundancy, or imbalance. Between 1982 and 1986, the Department of State sponsored a number of such reviews. The initiator of such reviews is usually the Office of Science and Technology policy in the White House. The agreements are still virtually in existence, an indication that there is generally acceptance of them. The 1986 Department of State report to the Congress on the science and technology relationship emphasized how the relationship has served overriding U.S. foreign policy objectives, and referred to discussions of joint efforts to be undertaken in the future.[19]

Factors that are already threatening the relationship from the Japanese point of view are: (1) anti-Japanese protectionism which is related to the deterioration of the world trade climate since the 1980; (2) the European protectionism against Japanese goods like video cassettes; (3) the increasing "voluntary" export restraints imposed on Japan by the United States; (4) in 1990 the imposition of tariffs on the Japanese semiconductor industry by the United States;[20] and (5) the increasing deemphasis on multilateralism in trade (disregard for GATT conventions) in favor of bilateral trade agreements. In sum, the Japanese view, and that of some influential observers, is that much of the retaliatory action in world politics has been directed at Japan. On the other hand, the Japanese are aware of some of their industrial policies put in place in the 1960s and 1970s, which are generating criticisms from other countries. Examples are the very limited acceptance of the certification by foreign factories of goods imported into Japan, and the delaying tactics employed by the Japanese bureaucracy when it comes to implementing various types of trade-liberalizing measures, among others. Japan's large trade surplus coupled with its unsavory trade practices have generated a great deal of dissatisfaction in Europe, Asia, and the United States; and in a continuous hardening of negative opinion among political and business leaders in these countries.

The United States has already started taking retaliatory measures against past Japanese protection of patents developed by its agencies. In 1983, for example, the United States introduced legislation that requires obtaining a waiver if a government patent is purchased by a firm that is producing a substantial amount of its product in foreign countries.[21] The Japanese are in fact the direct target of such protectionism because Japan has been a major purchaser of U.S. patents. As economies continue to compete for markets and conflicts increase, technonationalism as a mood will pervade the global economic relationship involving the advanced industrial countries—the United States, Japan, and Western Europe in particular.

Developments that will undermine the emergence of a pervasive mood of technonationalism directed against Japan are: instituting reforms in Japan that will make foreign licensing much easier. Joint efforts of Japanese and foreign researchers is one way of realizing this, a fact that has already been proposed by former Prime Minister Nakasone through his call for a Human Frontiers Science Program.[22] Second, another effective way to weaken tendencies toward technonationalism is by encouraging joint ventures between Japanese firms and foreign firms. The process will generate mutual access to technological innovations and mutual sharing of benefits. The Japanese subsidiary in another way, can participate in host country R&D efforts and eventually serve as agents of technological information transfer from overseas to Japan. Such measures in fact enhance positive cooperation and undermine the "adversarial" cooperation that is so often a key element of bilateral and even multilateral economic relationships.

The trade conflicts notwithstanding, the United States and Japan operate on the basis of recognized mutual interests and goals. The manifestation of mutual technological-dependence has been evident in the initiation of thirteen bilateral agreements since 1957. In his discussion of the Japanese Technical Literature Act of 1986, Mark Policinski underscored the significance of technological cooperation between the two countries and their joint focus on: (1) joint research with the objective of increasing the world's knowledge base; (2) enhancing the economic security of both countries by expanding the global economy; (3) enhancing the R&D capabilities within both countries; and (4) promoting mutual access to research results and improving reciprocity in exchange of personnel and use of research facilities.[23] The technological relationship is considered to be of such importance that one technological agreement was negotiated and implemented at the presidential level, the United States-Japan Agreement for cooperation in Research and Development in Science and Technology.

This beneficial interdependence of technology is increasingly reinforced by Japan's tremendous contribution to the United States technological base. Japan is now developing significant technology because of MITI-sponsored research projects and significant spending on R&D. The Japanese approach is a cooperative effort between Japanese industry and MITI. In particular, MITI selects a few key (very commercial potential) sectors and funds R&D in those sectors.[24] Additional resources are then supplied by the companies participating in the efforts. The results from such joint efforts are shared among the companies involved in the efforts.

However, as changes unfold in the international political economy, in particular in the relative economic strengths of the United States and Japan, the focus of reflection and analysis is whether the advanced industrial countries can continue the present "open" world economy—that is relatively free flow of trade and investment. This issue is analyzed, of course, in the light of a continuing U.S. hegemonic decline. Already, many observers express concern that the East-West military strategic rivalry is going to be replaced by an era of trade wars and neomercantilism. What can be said with any certainty is that the international economic order will continue to be guided by the leadership of one country, or a condominium of advanced industrial countries who benefit from an open economy. Collective cooperation to maintain an open economy would mean an accommodation of Japan's approach to macroeconomic and microeconomic management policies because of differences with those of the United States. For example, their assumptions regarding the relationship between government and firms differ. The United States spearheaded an international economy that separated macroeconomic management along Keynesian principles from the regulation of individual "micromarkets."

In terms of future scenarios, one outcome of Japan's response to limits placed on its international commercial activities could be to encourage the expansion of Japan's MNCs. The Japanese firm would then represent a solution to external pressures for more openness by Japan of its economy and retaliatory measures by the United States and other nations. Peter Cowhey expressed a similar view with regards to United States MNCs—to him they responded to many of the limits on trade created by many "closed" economies by encouraging foreign expansion.[25] Along the lines of containing such external economic imperatives, Japan exhibits three significant attributes. First, it has emphasized the merits of export-oriented growth. This focus is a strong factor in international macroeconomic policies, in particular exchange rate policies. This focus has also made Japan far more unwilling currently to assume an aggressive role in international growth efforts, although urged by the United States to do so. Second, Japan has stressed the advantages of national saving and investment over proconsumer policy behavior. Accordingly, the Japanese government has engaged in direct government oversight of investment flows, and implemented supply-side policies at the national level. Third, Japan has actively encouraged horizontal cooperation among its corporations in order to be competitive and to gain advantages in key industries through the management of economies of scale.

Japan has never accepted the United States separation of macroeconomic and microeconomic management. At the macroeconomic level Japan strongly favored supply-side policies that actively encouraged savings, penalized consumers, and focused on investment. The microeconomic policy behavior of Japan took the form of protecting export oligopolies and cartels from foreign competition and specific government policies for technology transfer and investment protection. The *keiretsu* is a system of elaborate ties between suppliers and consumers, and it is not merely simple sets of arrangements to exclude foreign goods and services.

The formulation of specific trade, technology, and research policies in Japan is always done through intensive consultation with industry associations. Just as MNC expansion is one way by which Japan tries to ease external criticisms and pressures, so also is the creation of such multinational production systems supposed to ease trade tensions. Networking is becoming a strong factor in such Japanese economic adaptation to a changing environment. For example, one venture that is thought to reduce United States-Japanese trade tensions was the recent MITI talks with industry concerning videocassette recorder (VCR) production in the United States. The talks focused on: (1) "a parts manufacturing center in the United States to be jointly owned by several Japanese VCR makers," (2) "encouraging Japanese VCR parts manufacturers to set up shop in the United States," (3) "offering technological assistance to American firms" who supply parts for Japanese VCRs.[26]

Finally, as the economic policy convergence between the United States and Japan increases, their management styles with regard to world order will become more pervasive. The current competing structures of technological trade and investment will be modified further in response to frictions. The objective should be a mutually acceptable balance of technological power between the two nations.

Summary

This examination of the unfolding dynamics of the United States-Japan technological relationship like many other issue-areas underscores the combined effect of three interactive dimensions: a structural dimension (ongoing changes in the relative technological capabilities of the two nations); a procedural dimension (ongoing changes in the institutions and procedures around which the two nations expectations on technological issues converge, and a "substantive" dimension (changes in the actual bilateral expectations of the two nations on science and technology issues). The turbulence in the technological relationship between the two nations corresponds with a growing perception of a fundamental disequilibrium in the international technological system threatening an increasing dislocation between the norms and expectations governing technological exchange and the relative distribution of technological power.

The analysis in this book suggests that there is a turbulence of sorts in the Japanese-American relationship manifested in the various issue-areas: trade, technology, military security, foreign aid, and so on. The upheaval has been generated by the shift from a stable United States hegemonic leadership, or Japan's hegemonic dependence on the United States, to a growing trend of mutual power-dependence between the two nations. Technonationalism, an aspect of economic nationalism, in fact constitutes one of the pressing issues on the Japanese-American agenda. The crisis of sorts seems to originate in the differing public policies of the two nations regarding technology—a United States emphasis on basic research and a Japanese focus on process and production technology. Second, the crisis in the relationship is further strengthened by the culture incompatibilities between the two countries, defining "fair" and "unfair" practices in technological or scientific relations between the two countries is a complex issue.

The differences in approach, notwithstanding, many analysts contend that in the evolving new global economic order characterized by convergence among advanced industrial countries, both American and Japanese firms can equally benefit from new knowledge resulting from R&D activity in both countries. Technological parity thus means expanded opportunities for mutual trade in knowledge and products. In other words, technological leadership is becoming an obsolete notion in a world of complex interdependence and multilateral linkages where the national agenda is an integral part of the global agenda and *vice versa*. Adhering to this non zero-sum view of technological competition could result in a decrease in technological frictions and serve as a key factor in raising the well-being of all.

Endnotes

1 For facts and figures on the comparative assessment of the U.S.-Japan science and technology relationship, see, "Japan 1985: An International Comparison," (Tokyo: Keizai Koho Center, 1985); National Science Board, *Science Indicators The 1985 Report* (Washington D.C.: National Science Board, 1985); and George Thomas Kurian, *Facts on File, National Profiles, Japan* (New York: Facts on File Inc., 1990).

2 For further details on the evolution of science and technology in Japan, see account by Yoshimitsu Takeyasu, "Science and Technology Policy in Japan," in Cecil H. Uyehara (ed.) *U.S.-Japan Science and Technology Exchange* (Boulder: Westview Press, 1988) pp. 178–187.

3 Cecil H. Uyehara (ed.), *U.S.-Japan Technological Exchange Symposium* (Washington D.C.: University Press of America, 1982) p. 54.

4 For a more thorough discussion of American technological and managerial development, see, Alfred Dupont Chandler, *The Visible Hand: The Managerial Revolution in American Business* (Cambridge: Harvard University Press, 1977).

5 Further historical analysis is found in Richard N. Nelson, (ed.) *Government and Technical Progress: A Cross-Industry Analysis* (New York: Pergamon Press, 1982).

6 For further details on these measures, see, National Science Board, *Science Indicators: The 1985 Report* (Washington, D.C.: U.S. Government Printing Office, 1985).

7 Richard R. Nelson, "What Has Happened to U.S. Technological Leadership?" in Gunter Heiduk and Kozo Yamamura (eds.), *Technological Competition and Interdependence* (Seattle: University of Washington Press, 1990) pp. 3–24.

8 For further details, see, "Japan's U.S. R&D Role Widens, Begs Attention," *Science* (July 18, 1986): 270–272; and "High Technology, Clash of Titans," *The Economist* (August 23, 1986).

9 Justin L. Bloom," A New Era of U.S.-Japanese Technical Relations? A Cloudy Vision," in Cecil H. Uyehara (ed.) *U.S.-Japan Science and Technology Exchange* (Boulder: Westview Press, 1988) pp. 219–254.

10 A distinction is made here between the two because the former refers to a similarity or congruence of value positions not underpinned by competition or rivalry; whereas the latter has a game-theoretic derivative that focuses on the common interest of rivals or adversaries regardless of conflicting values and

objectives. For more details, see, Thomas C. Schelling, *Strategy of Conflict* (New York: Oxford University Press, 1960); and Robert Axelrod, *The Evolution of Cooperation* (New York: Basic Books, 1984).

11 United States-Japan Advisory Commission, *Challenges and Opportunities in United States-Japan Relations: A Report Submitted to the President of the United States and the Prime Minister of Japan* (Washington D.C.: United States-Japan Advisory Commission, September 1984) p. 97.

12 Gerald P. Dinneen, "U.S.-Japanese Science and Technology: A Comparative Assessment," in Cecil H. Uyehara (ed.), *U.S.-Japan Science and Technology Exchange*, (Boulder: Westview Press, 1988) pp. 1–28.

13 Science and Technology Agency, *Indicators of Science and Technology* (1984) (Tokyo: STA, March 30, 1985) pp. 138–140.

14 Martha Harris, "Japan's International Technology Transfers," *Japan's economy and trade with the United States* (Washington, D.C.: Joint Economic Committee, Congress of the United States, December 9, 1985) pp. 114–142.

15 For data and further insights into the trade imbalance between the two countries, see, "Japan's U.S. R&D Role Widens, Begs Attention," *Science* (July 18, 1986): 270–272; and U.S. Department of Commerce, International Trade Association, 1986, *U.S. Industrial Outlook* (Washington, D.C.: U.S. Government Printing Office, 1986).

16 See, National Science Foundation, "International Science and Technology Data Update, 1986" (Directorate for Scientific, Technological, and International Affairs, Division of Science Resource Studies, 1986), p. 54; and U.S. Department of Commerce, *United States Trade: Performance in 1985 and Outlook* (Washington, D.C.: U.S. Department of Commerce, International Trade Administration, October 1986) p. 131.

17 For details on arguments along these lines, see, Rachel McColloch, "The Challenge to U.S. Leadership in High Technology Industries: Can the United States Maintain Its Lead? Should It Try?" in Gunter Heiduk and Kozo Yamamura (eds.) *Technological Competition and Interdependence* (Seattle: University of Washington Press, 1990) pp. 192–211; Susan Strange, "Still an Extraordinary Power: America's Role in a Global Monetary System," in Raymond E. Lombra and William Witte, *Political Economy of International and Domestic Monetary Relations* (Ames: Iowa State University Press, 1982); and Bruce Russett, "The Mysterious Case of Vanishing Hegemony: or is Mark Twain Really Dead?" *International Organization* XXXIX, No. 2 (Spring 1985): 207–234.

18 For further details, see, Daniel Okimoto and Gary Saxonhouse, "Technology and the Future of the Economy," in Kozo Yamamura and Yasukichi Yasuka (eds.), *The Political Transformation* (Stanford, Calif.: Stanford University Press, 1987); and OECD *Science and Technology Indicators* (Paris OECD, Annual Series).

19 See, *Science, Technology, and U.S. Diplomacy, 1986*, Seventh annual report submitted to the Congress by the president pursuant to Section 503(b) of Title V of Public Law 95–426 (Washington, D.C.: U.S. Government Printing Office, May 1986) p. 38.

20 See, for example, "Japan's Closed Door Brings Hard Knocks," *Wall Street Journal*, 16 April 1987.

21 See, Gary Saxonhouse, "Industrial Policy and Factor Markets," in Hugh Patrick (ed.), *Japan's High Technology Industries* (Seattle: University of Washington Press, 1986) p. 130.

22 "Nakasone Nurtures Vision of Sponsoring Ground-Breaking Scientific Research," *Asian Wall Street Journal*, 13 October 1986.

23 Mark R. Policinski, "The Japanese Technical Literature Act of 1986," in Cecil H. Uyehara (ed.) *U.S.-Japan Science and Technology Exchange* (Boulder: Westview Press, 1988) pp. 57–61.

24 For details on the sectors funded, see, G. Turrin, et al., *JTECH Panel Report on Telecommunications Technology in Japan* (La Jolla, Calif.: Science Applications International Corporation, May 1986).

25 Peter F. Cowhey, "The Agenda of the Leading nations for the World Economy: A Theory of International Regimes," Gunter Heiduk and Kozo Yamamura (eds.), *Technological Competition and Interdependence* (Seattle: University of Washington Press, 1990) pp. 107–147.

26 As quoted in the *Japan economic journal*, 20 June 1987, p. 4.

UNITED STATES-JAPAN MUTUAL SECURITY INTERFACE

As dramatic changes in the international system destabilize the structural and procedural elements on which the stability of the liberal international economic order is dependent, so also do issues in the global agenda undergo transformation. The primacy of the nuclear weapons *problematique* is rapidly being matched by the growing priority given to low politics issues—the environment, trade, finance, and the like. Accordingly, efforts have been expended by scholars of late to redefine and reconceptualize security.[1] The frequent reference to "alternative security" has thus tended to present a melange of, and appropriately underscore the complex interconnectedness of, economic and military security, instead of just narrowly focusing on military security issues usually embodied in discussions of the concept of national security.

This analysis of American-Japanese security in the context of challenge to the postwar American hegemonic leadership will be approached from two dimensions: military-strategic defensive issues, and their interface with economic security and high technology. The two countries are, in other words, linked by an interdependence of military and economic issues manifested in many areas of conflict and cooperation. Forty percent of Japanese exports go to the United States, and Japan relies on the United States for military security. The United States looks to Japan for increased technology sharing because Japan leads in some areas of technology and will lead in more in the coming years. In particular, Japan's reliance on America's extended deterrent capability illustrates the lingering hegemonic dependence, while the American concern for security in LDCs which has generated pressures on Japan to do more on behalf of global order and development, illustrates an aspect of mutual power-dependence. On the one hand, developing regions are a source of security concern for both the United States and

Japan, and on the other hand, they are sources of raw material supply or export markets and therefore important to security calculations. Japan's cooperation with LDCs is assumed to strengthen the United States-Japanese security cooperation. The United States is itself officially recognizing the evolving major military security status of Japan. In early 1988, an advisory commission to the National Security Council and Defense Department emphasized the critical role that Japan will play in future United States strategic planning.[2] In sum, as changes unfold in the global system, it is worth reflecting on the evolving patterns of United States-Japanese security behavior.

Hegemonic Security Interdependence

During the 1950s, in particular, Japan had little or no global responsibilities and made very little effort to internationalize its activities. The policy decisions that it formulated were either subordinate or complementary to those of the United States. But now the relationship has developed into one of bilateral interdependence, or more precisely a relationship of mutual power-dependence with the United States. While Japan still shelters under the umbrella of America's nuclear deterrent, it nonetheless is increasingly assuming United States regional responsibilities in strategic countries like Egypt, Pakistan, Turkey, and Yemen, among others. Japan's policy decisions and the force of its economy continue to have a tremendous impact on the United States and the entire liberal international economic order. The ongoing relationship of mutual power-dependence results in frictions over trade and in complaints by the United States over an imbalance in defense burden sharing. The frictions and disagreements are, of course, predicated on competing national interests.

Irrespective of the mood in the entire United States-Japan relationship, Japanese leaders have consistently emphasized the indispensable role of the United States as an ally and at the same time view a continued strong United States as essential for Japan's future. They also consistently reiterate their determination (perhaps because of America's relative decline and pressure) to share the responsibilities of partnership with the United States and discharge fully their global responsibilities. Accordingly, Prime Minister Noboru Takeshita in 1988 announced concrete measures geared towards an increased contribution by Japan to the world. The global cooperation initiative consists of three main pillars: (1) the strengthening of Japan's contribution to peace; (2) promote international cultural exchanges; and (3) expand Japan's ODA. Japan reiterated its past policy option of not seeking to be a military power and not playing a military role in the world.[3] On the other hand, Japan is resolved to contribute to world peace through active involvement in international efforts to resolve and prevent conflicts. Japan cooperated with other nations to help guarantee safe navigation in the Persian Gulf during the Iran-Iraq War. In 1988 Japan offered funds to the Multinational force and observers in the Sinai Peninsula which help maintain peace between Israel and Egypt. Afghanistan and Namibia were among the regional conflicts that Japan rendered assistance to either in the form of financial aid or participation in an international civilian observer team. More recently, Japan also participated in the Persian Gulf War even to the point of almost violating the constraints imposed by Article 9 of its Constitution.

However, some United States policy makers believe that Japan needs to do more to beef up its defenses, especially with regards to security in the Far East. In 1988, during the Soviet military buildup in the Far East, it was argued that Japan should not aim only at meeting its minimum security requirements. United States policymakers called for, among other things: hardening Japanese bases and upgrading communications between United States and Japanese forces; providing greater sustainability for the Self-Defense Forces; further cooperation on arms procurement such as with the FSX; expanding Japanese support of American forces stationed there; and more expenditure on development to meet the one percent of GNP target in the light of decreasing levels of United States assistance, that would advance their (United States and Japan) common interests.[4]

The American pressure on Japan is largely a reflection of the spillover of American economic insecurity to military insecurity. In general, American insecurity stems largely from its loss of the international competitiveness it enjoyed in the liberal international economic order prior to the 1970s. In particular, it has over the years lost comparative advantage in textiles, steel, household electronics, automobiles, and now even in many categories of high technology industries. Besides, United States world trade has since 1971 almost consistently registered a deficit, with its trade deficit with Japan reaching the $58 billion mark.[5] Furthermore, in 1987 United States high technology trade slipped into the red for the first time in the postwar era. The consequence is a United States openly adhering to freer trade principles while its insecurity over the decline makes it increasingly resort to pressure tactics to get Japan to engage in more economic and military burden sharing.

In the immediate post-World War II era, the hegemonic leadership of the United States provided a refuge in which Japan could focus almost exclusively on its own foreign economic and overall domestic objectives. This situation enabled Japan to adhere to the constraints imposed by the no-war clause in its constitution. This, in particular, translated into limiting its defense spending to one percent of its GNP, prohibiting weapons export, avoiding collective security arrangements, limiting its Self-Defense Forces to strictly defensive functions, and maintaining its adherence to the three non-nuclear principles. Second, the United States hegemonic umbrella shielded Japan from all the pressures for burden sharing commensurate with its position in the international system.

The safety of the refuge ended in the 1970s. This situation forced Japan to search first for "economic security" and then for "comprehensive security." The 1970s just as the late 1980s produced some rather disturbing effects that in one way or the other affected Japan: the United States-Soviet detente of 1969 to 1979, and their strategic nuclear parity; the Sino-American rapprochement; Nixon's "New Economic Policy" which was one indicator of the virtual collapse of the Bretton Woods Economic System; the growing Sino-Soviet rift; the oil crises of 1973 and 1979; the United States policy of substantial military retrenchment from Southeast Asia as reflected in the Guam Doctrine; and the United States defeat in the Vietnam War. The Chinese and Vietnam incidents particularly worried the Japanese in terms of the United States resolve to keep its commitments. The U.S.-PRC normalization of relations further raised doubts about United States reliability and alliance stability, particularly since it favored the PRC over Taiwan regardless of existing treaties.[6] The early 1980s also presented Japan with serious events of significant impact on its security concerns. Among other things, were the disruption of Gulf maritime transportation by the Iran-Iraq War, the Vietnamese invasion of Cambodia and China's "military conflict" with Vietnam, and the Soviet invasion of Afghanistan.

In the early 1980s, calls for more Japanese involvement in security spending was motivated by strategic considerations, in particular, the expansion of Soviet military strength in the Far East. To give directions to their security cooperation the United States and Japan in June 1981 agreed on the following ground rules: (1) continuation of a credible United States nuclear deterrent and an offensive strike force in the Northwest Pacific; (2) Japanese responsibility for the security and protection of its territory, coastal waters, air space, vital sea lanes of commerce up to about 1,000 miles from its pacific seaports; and (3) continuation of United States security commitment to the republic of Korea and protection of its sea lanes beyond the Northwest Pacific critical to Japan's security such as oil routes.[7] Related to the changing security environment and its relationship with the United States, Japan has since 1984 steadily increased its defense budget annually. There has been an annual increase of approximately six percent since Fiscal Year 1983 to become the sixth largest military budget in the world.[8]

A major obstacle to overt and extensive military buildup for Japan is Article 9, the no-war clause in the United States-drafted Constitution. Although many Japanese dislike the substantial United States influence in the constitution, many Japanese on the left and right, nonetheless, support Article 9 because it inhibits any growth in militarism and excessive defense expenditure. The result is in part Japan's continuing no-defense inertia caused by its traditional security dependence on the United States, and in part by Japan's economic self-interest.

Edward Olsen in his analysis of United States-Japan security relationship divided Japan's postwar strategic thinking into four categories: emotional pacifism, pragmatic pacifism, emotional nationalism, and pragmatic nationalism.[9] The pacific aspect of Japan's foreign policy and defense behavior emanates from its defeat in World War II, its constitutional constraints expressed in Article 9 of the Constitution, and its "free rider" behavior motivated by its inclusion in the United States nuclear umbrella and United States proxy role on its behalf. Its nationalism is manifested in its reluctance to succumb to United States pressures to increase its defense commitments, among other things.

Its pacifism, notwithstanding, Japan has been an integral part of United States strategic policy in Asia since the end of World War II. In the late 1970s and 1980s the United States tried to involve Japan in more strategic cooperation by underscoring the Soviet threat. The United States emphasized tangible factors like: expansion of the Soviet Pacific Fleet; Soviet troop emplacements on island off Hokkaido, Japan's northernmost islands; Soviet moves during the Cold War to offset United States installations in the Philippines through transformation of the former United States naval facility at Cam Rahn Bay, Vietnam; and Soviet direct interventionist behavior in Asia such as its invasion of Afghanistan. The current

Japanese security issue is the return of the islands occupied by the former Soviet Union since World War II.

For a long time and even now both the United States and Japan overall adhere to overlapping but at the same time different world views. Japan is generally pacifist in orientation with strong overtones of nationalism. The United States is inherently globalist with constant preoccupation with the maintenance of global and regional balances. Japan in the 1950s and even now, to still a large extent, operates on the *seikei bunri* policy—separating economic concerns from political concerns and largely focusing on the former. By the 1970s Japan shifted gradually into an internationalist (globalist) posture largely abandoning *sekei bunri*. The objective of *Zenhoi heiwa gaiko*—"omnidirectional peaceful diplomacy"—according to Prime Minister Takeo Fukuda, was to maintain friendly relations with as many nations as possible to avoid any political waves that might damage Japan's global economic interests.

The persistence of Japan's non-military worldview and its cautious adaptation to changing times was reflected in its Summer 1980 *Report on Comprehensive National Security*.[10] This report of a private advisory body established by Prime Minister Ohira concluded that Japan could best contribute to the security burden by becoming more active in the political, economic, and military fronts, but called for more emphasis to be given to economic skills. It reiterated Japan's policy pattern of minimizing military contributions and playing only a supportive role in military issues because of constitutional constraints. The next sections of this analysis focus on the goals of Japan's comprehensive security policy as they affect the conflictual and cooperative relationship with the United States, and the trend of Japan's adaptive security reflex in an emerging multipolar system.

Economic and Military Security Interface

The post-World War II United States-Japan bilateral relationship in fact embodies a substantial degree of economic, political, and military security interface. Japan's concept of "comprehensive security" first introduced in 1982 is designed to enhance security by focusing on three levels: an emphasis on self-help or self-defense; the maintenance of an acceptable balance of power in the international system—that is render the international system conducive to Japan's security; and a promotion of security cooperation especially with the United

States—that is a focus on regional security to ensure peace in the immediate environment.[11] The three levels are further designed to contain various types of political, military, and economic national security threats. The vehicles of containment thus include both defense buildup and economic aid to developing countries to reduce political instability especially in the Asian region.

Japan, in response to security threats emanating from developing regions has already exhibited a great deal of either independence or cooperative reflex to enhance its overall security. With the threat of the 1973–74 oil crisis, Tokyo made serious efforts to reduce its dependence on Middle Eastern oil. This instance of Japanese vulnerability coupled with other security threatening events—the Iran-Iraq War and its effects on the Persian Gulf, the Vietnam invasion of Cambodia, the China-Vietnam military skirmishes, and the Soviet invasion of Afghanistan had a significant impact on Japan's decision to embrace a policy of "comprehensive security"—that is a broader approach to national and regional security. In the Iran-Iraq War Japan was made to realize that it was now expected to contribute directly to contain regional conflicts that threatened the international system. Japan was heavily criticized by the United States and other Western allies for not contributing directly to multilateral military efforts to limit the effect of the conflict on the supply of oil.

In the United States-Japan security cooperation, the United States views itself as having global responsibilities, whereas Japan is viewed as the most important element in the Asian strategy of the Western alliance. According to Japan playing this role does not require an expanded security role or increasing the defense budget to two percent of GNP, a goal advocated by some Americans. But with the relative economic decline of the United States vis-a-vis Japan and Western Europe, the impression is being conveyed that Japan holds the key to a significant reduction in American military spending.[12] In the first year of the Reagan Administration the two countries assessed their security cooperation. The United States reaffirmed its intent to shoulder the responsibility of extending its nuclear deterrent to Japan, to secure the northwest Pacific, and to protect sea-lanes vital to Japan in the southwest Pacific and the Indian Ocean. Japan, in turn, agreed to the defense of its territory, air, and sea-lane out to 1,000 nautical miles.

Japan as a result of its defensive posture views the United states military presence and effective deterrent in the Western Pacific as essential to peace and stability in Asia and the Pacific. The United States troops stationed in Japan under the Japan-United States security arrangement are considered a significant contribution to the security not only of Japan but also of the Far East. Similarly, Japan's cooperation with LDCs is assumed to strengthen United States-Japanese security cooperation. The three international cooperation initiatives serve as a basis for Japan's relations with regions of the Third World as well as ASEAN countries. Economic cooperation is designed to play a central role in Japan-Third World relations, and the expansion of ODA is the centerpiece of this relationship, one of the three pillars of the international cooperation initiative.

Japan's increasing globalist and security-oriented behavior is manifested in large part in its global cooperation initiatives and enhanced by United States Congressional attitudes. In September 1987, the United States Senate adopted a resolution entitled: "*Sense of the Congress Stability,*" which stated that Japan should increase its ODA to about 3 percent of GNP by 1992. During the same period, a joint congressional conference adopted a resolution calling on Japan to increase its total for ODA and defense spending to a level close to the average for NATO countries by 1992. Japan now spends about 1.6 percent of GNP using the NATO formula for calculating defense expenditure including military pensions and the like. In 1988, West European NATO nations spent an average of about 3.5 percent of GNP on ODA and defense combined.[13]

In security terms, Japan's response to the Soviet invasion of Afghanistan converged with, and complemented, that of the United States and its other allies. Japan participated fully in diplomatic protests, economic sanctions, increased defense buildups, boycott of the Moscow Olympics, increased security cooperation with the United States, and suspended all joint Soviet-Japanese projects for the development of Siberian natural resources. The American-Japanese security cooperation elicited by Soviet expansionist behavior culminated in Tokyo's decision to expand its maritime defense capabilities and eliminate its post 1976 defense spending ceiling of one percent of GNP. In such politico-military security cooperation with the United States and other allies, Japan is expressing its willingness to translate its enormous power economic capabilities into power political and perhaps even military influence.

The military dimension of Japan's comprehensive security is now and again brought into focus as crisis situations erupt that threaten Japan's access to strategic raw materials, or as regional instability tends to threaten its territorial integrity. For example, the recent Persian Gulf War forced many Japanese, including the

Japanese government to question the relevance of the no-war clause in their constitution. The military dimension of security policy has in fact been undergoing changes, and of late it has experienced some serious challenges emanating largely from the external environment.

In May 1957, the "Basic Policy for National Defense" was adopted with the emphasis that the objective of Japan's national defense is to prevent and repel aggression and preserve the independence of Japan. According to the government, it is illegal for Japan to deploy armed forces in foreign lands for the purpose of using force. Japan is prohibited from exercising the right of collective self-defense. But the use of the Self-Defense Forces for self-defense purposes is constitutional. These limits were put on trial during the Persian Gulf crisis. In August 1990, the government pledged that between 100 to 200 medical personnel would be sent to the Gulf as a first step in Japan's contribution to the war effort. Prime Minister Kaifu next unveiled a proposed United Nations Peace Cooperation Corps, a mechanism for Japanese personnel to participate in the multinational force in non-combat support roles. The struggle within Japan next focused on the constitutionality of including portions of the Self Defense Forces in the corps. The debate revolved around whether overseas deployment of unarmed SDF elements would be tantamount to merely the sending of personnel (*haken*) or the unconstitutional dispatch of troops (*hahei*). Prime Minister Kaifu himself argued that the dispatch of SDF forces for purposes of collective defense (*shudan boei*) would be unconstitutional, but that their dispatch for participation in collective security functions (*shudanteki anzen hosho*) would be strictly constitutional. Eventually, Kaifu was forced to abandon the idea of a United Nations Peace Corps because of certain Diet rejection. Japan resorted, instead, in January 1991, to pledge an additional $9 billion to the allied effort.[14]

Bilateral security relations between Japan and the United States are an integral part of Japan's comprehensive security policy. Japan works hard to enhance its bilateral arrangements with the United States because it views the United States-Japan security system as the foundation of its national security policy. Close consultation on security matters between the two nations are held under the umbrella of the Mutual Security Treaty. In January 1950, the first forum for consultation was created, and usually brings together the Japanese Foreign Minister and Defense Agency Director General and the United States Ambassador to Japan and the Commander-in-Chief of the United States Pacific

Command. Other forums include: the Security Consultative Committee; the Security Subcommittee; the Security Consultative Group; and the Japan-United States Joint Committee.[15] In addition to these joint meetings, joint studies also focus on joint defense planning, sea-lane defense, the Japan-United States defense coordination center, and intelligence exchange, among others. The SDFs also engage in joint military training with United States forces in the areas of anti-submarine and minesweeping, and command post exercises, among others.

The United States-Japan mutual power-dependence examined in the previous chapter is also increasingly manifested in their security relationship—cooperation in the field of military equipment and technology. The United States has transferred to Japan such weapons as surface-to-air missiles (SAMs) and C-130H transport aircraft, as part of the United States Foreign Military Sales (FMS) program. Since the mid 1950s, a series of United States aircraft have been produced in Japan under licensing agreements with companies such as Lockheed. The relationship of weapons technology transfer has shifted from being totally one-sided (United States to Japan) to being reciprocal. In particular, the level of Japanese technological sophistication has prompted the United states to request weapons technology transfer to the United States. In response, Japan decided in 1983 to slightly relax its policy prohibiting arms export by exempting the transfer of dual-purpose technologies to the United States. With further agreements concluded in 1985, Japan has approved the transfer to the United States of SAM-related technology, technology relevant to the construction of naval vessels, and technology relevant to the modification of United States naval vessels.

The transformation of Japan's power economic capabilities into politico-military influence continues and is increasingly manifested in joint technological efforts with the United States and consequently in a gradual relaxation of its no-war clause, non nuclear principles, and other self-imposed military policies. For example, Japan decided in 1986 to cooperate with the United States in the SDI program with the understanding that its objective was to create a "sophisticated non-nuclear defensive system" whose ultimate objective was the elimination of the nuclear weapons threat. Within Japan, the Japanese government bears the burden of supporting United States soldiers stationed there, at a cost of $45,000 per U.S. soldier. Since, 1979 Japan has expanded its obligations to the United States Forces, Japan (USFJ) to include improvement of their living quarters and labor related costs. In sum, Japan is involved in extremely cooperative activities related to its own defense and to the presence of the United States Forces in Japan.

In the area of security, a fundamental fact about Japan's strategic evolution is that the nation's extensive global economic power projection is occasionally challenged by volatile and explosive regional situations like the recent Gulf War, the Iran-Iraq War, and the 1973–74 oil crisis generated by the Yom Kippur War. Events like these have led Japan to the conclusion that a search for "economic security" is insufficient and should therefore be replaced by a focus on "comprehensive security." As we have repeatedly emphasized, economic power often translates into global involvements and at times even regional entanglements. The reality of Japan's economic power has led the government to expand its economic contribution to peace and security, especially those of the Asian-Pacific region. This globalist and activist role originated with the Nakasone administration, and was consolidated by the Takeshita administration. Prime Minister Noboru Takeshita's foreign policy was predicated on these four basic principles: (1) to maintain continuity in Japan's diplomacy; (2) to launch Japan on an independent foreign policy based on its own will and initiative; (3) to place the highest priority on strengthening the United States-Japanese relationship; and (4) to increase Japan's contribution to the world.[16] Accordingly, in 1988 Takeshita announced an "International Cooperation Initiative," which has since been upheld by his successors—Susuko Uno, Toshiki Kaifu, and now Kiichi Miyazawa. The Initiative is based on three strategies: expansion of ODA; promotion of international cultural exchange; and strengthening of Japan's contribution to international peace. Foreign aid as a component of the Initiative has already been discussed extensively in chapter three of this book.

Japan's multilateral role is rapidly expanding such that Japan currently contributes almost ten percent of the total member contributions to the United Nations agencies, second only to the United States which contributes about 17 percent.[17] Japan's contributions to international peace is supposed to take the form of: an active diplomatic role in resolving regional conflicts; and providing funds and civilian personnel for United Nations peace-keeping activities. Japan currently contributes over 11 percent of the total member contributions to United Nation peacekeeping organizations. The United States and the former Soviet Union contribute 30 percent and 12 percent respectively. An integral part of regional wars and peace-keeping is the refugee situation in various parts of the world. Japan's unfolding globalism has also responded to the efforts of the United Nations High Commissioner for Refugees (UNHCR) and the United Nations Relief and Works Agency (UNRWA) by contributing more than $70 million to the two agencies. Refugee and reconstruction programs received a total of $259 million from the Takeshita government.[18] The funds were targeted at Afghan refugees, the Palestinian support project under the United Nations Development Program (UNDP) and the Multinational Force and Observers (MFO) on the Sinai Peninsula. In addition, Japanese government officials participated in the United Nations Good Offices Mission in Afghanistan and Pakistan (UNGOMAP) and the United Nations Iran-Iraq Military Observer Group (UNIIMOG), the United Nations Transition Group (UNTAG) in Namibia, and the Kampuchea War, and in the 1991 Gulf War, Japan dispatched SDF aircraft to the Gulf for the evacuation of afflicted refugees.

This use of power economic (financial) capabilities to help alleviate political and military problems stems from a realization that effective economic power projection is not possible without a stable politico-military environment. Thus, its economic resources are being used as instruments to guarantee a stable global economic order. Official Development Assistance is the key foundation of Japan's push for globalism and hence its comprehensive security strategy. In terms of Comprehensive Security, Japan's ODA philosophy comprises of four rationales: (1) Japan must contribute to international security as a member of international society who has renounced the war options; (2) as an economic superpower, Japan is expected to contribute to the establishment of a North-South order; (3) Japan's ODA can be instrumental in reducing its vulnerability stemming from its foreign dependence; and (4) as a non-western nation, Japan must respond even more to expectations that Asian developing nations have for the country.

Japan's economic resources and its push for globalism assume enormous importance when viewed in terms of the fact that United States financial resources are increasingly diminishing. Ninety percent of United States aid ($14.6 billion in 1990) was targeted at a small group of about 15 countries.[19] Besides, most of the aid is military. The reality of diminished United States economic aid and Washington's overall budget woes, severely limit America's ability to effectively and credibly respond to the demands of the evolving democracies of Eastern Europe, Latin America, and Africa. The United States, has thus, often resorted to pressure tactics directed at its allies, in particular Japan.

The Changing Parameters of Security Concerns

The United States-Japan security cooperation now and again experiences troubled moments especially in the area of high technology. What some experts have referred to as "technonationalism"—the charge that one is trying to hold back the other's progress and maintain some sort of lead in the high technology race. As the security cooperation unfolds in coming years, both countries will have to deal with this increasing area of friction—the determination of both countries to pursue technological hegemony.[20] There have been some notable examples of technonationalist clashes. Under pressure from Eastman Kodak company, the University of Rochester Business School rejected a Japanese student in August 1987 on the grounds that classroom discussions would be inhibited in his presence. Fujitsu Corporation, Japan's largest computer maker, was discouraged by the Commerce Department and the Pentagon from acquiring the troubled Fairchild Corporation, even though Fairchild was already owned by the French-controlled Schlumberger Corporation.

The year 1987 stands out prominently as one characterized by both technonationalism and/or trade frictions involving measures taken by the United States Congress. In December 1987, United States legislators attached a reciprocity amendment to the omnibus spending package that prohibits Japanese and other foreign construction firms from participating in federally funded public works projects in the United States. In 1987 the Presidency, for the first time since World War II also entered the assault against Japan. President Reagan imposed the harshest economic sanctions against Japan in March 1987 when he ordered $300 million worth of tariffs on certain Japanese imports in retaliation for Japanese violations of the 1986 semiconductor accord.

Thus, there are growing fears that America would lose to Japan even in high technology. Such a loss will have two implications for American security concerns: (1) easier non-western access to advanced technologies through Japan; and (2) a further slide in United States economic decline since high technology is considered essential in revitalizing the United States economy. The overall consequence for the United States will be an arms race with potential non-western countries on the one hand, and a technological catch up game with the Japanese on the other. A battle on two fronts (military and economic) may not be helpful for a country already in relative decline. This security concern was reflected in the intervention by the United States Department of Defense in 1983 against

Nippon Steel's plan to acquire Special Metals Allegheny International, the 1984 DOD attempt to prevent Mineba from acquiring New Hampshire Ball Bearings, and the 1987 United States opposition to Fujistu's plan to purchase Fairchild Semiconductor from Schlumberger, as well as the tough United States action on the alleged Japanese violations of the bilateral semiconductor agreement.

There are even some in the United States Congress who are cautions about technological exchange with Japan. For example, in the issue of the Aegis sale to Japan in early 1988, the House Armed Services Seapower and Strategic and Critical Materials Subcommittee met in February to consider legislation that would prevent the DOD from selling the latest weapons system to Japan. The Reagan Administration, on the other hand, believed that selling the system to Japan would enhance the security of the Pacific region, and also be in the overall interest of the United States.[21] Many American policy makers think that the way to establish balance between the United States-Japanese security responsibilities is for Japan to play a larger economic role in developing nations. Many have proposed that Japan concentrate on Third World development as a way to balance economic relationships. In December 1987, the United States Congress enacted a resolution urging Japan to increase its foreign aid to the average level of defense expenditures by the European allies.

In the area of defense burden sharing, the United States House Armed Services Committees's special burdensharing panel on August 6, 1988 released its interim report on allied contributions to the common defense. The report charged that "Europe and Japan are not contributing or producing security resources commensurate with their economic ability to pay or their vital interests in keeping with their homelands."[22] The United States Senate, in turn, in its fiscal year 1989 defense appropriations bill contained several burdensharing measures that target Japan. The change in United States behavior is obviously due to fiscal constraints posed by the growing large budget deficits. Among other things, the United States burdensharing panel suggested that Japan increase its ODA substantially and target more aid to countries, such as Turkey and the Philippines, that have economic needs and strategic importance to both the United States and Japan. Such pressure followed the February 1988 Armed Services Committee conclusion that the United State has reached the stage where it is incapable of simultaneously acting to police the world and build a strong and stable economy. The chair of the Committee, Representative Patricia Schroeder, summed up the issue when she said: "We can no longer shoulder the burden of defending our NATO allies and Japan without a greater commitment from them for their own defense. Our future security rests in a growing domestic economy and competitiveness in international markets."[23]

However, the constant United States pressure on Japan for an expanded defense role is undermined by certain factors. First, many in Japan would argue that their mission is to defend the Japanese home islands and adjacent sea-lanes. Second, they do not view it as part of their global role to send military forces to other regions such as the Persian Gulf or other parts of the Middle East. Third, the Japanese have a strong aversion to nuclear weapons because of Hiroshima and Nagasaki. Fourth, any expanded military-strategic regional role would be met by vigorous opposition from other Asian countries. For example, many Asian countries reacted negatively when Japan's defense budget exceeded one percent of GNP. Finally, the major security threat the Soviet Union is no longer in existence.

A more forthright commitment to globalism in general and security cooperation emerged with Prime Minister Nakasone. The Prime Minister seemed to have been going against the pattern of thought still prevalent in Japan regarding security commitments. His commitment to more Japanese burden sharing and global commitment was captured in this analogy: "Japan used to live in a small house, but now that it has moved into a larger house, it must pay a larger insurance premium. Should we not realize this fact? Defense spending, in a sense, is something like an insurance premium we pay, just in case."[24] In a speech delivered in August 1983, he called upon Japan to play a more active role in global affairs. His rhetoric was at least quite different from that of past Japanese Prime Ministers. In particular, during his visit to the United States in 1983, at the May 28-30 Williamsburg Summit he made an offer to share arms technology. Three months later in a speech to the Diet, Nakasone said:

> Exchanging defense technologies with the United States has become very important in ensuring an effective operation of the Japan-United States security arrangement. In view of its importance, the government has decided as part of two-way exchanges, to open the way for providing weapons technology to the United States within the framework of pertinent provision of the Japan-United States mutual defense assistance agreement. According to the decision, the three principles concerning the export of arms will not be applicable in this case.[25]

In spite of this comprehensive security commitment, more pressures have been emanating from the United States. The pressures are closely related to the continuing high trade deficit and related United States economic problems. Within Congress, the proclivity exists to link security and economic issues. The argument is that Japan should increase defense spending because it runs a huge trade surplus with the United States. The emphasis is not on the external threat but on economic relations with the United States. Some in the United States government, on the other hand, consider the linkage argument as unreasonable because they take into account the effect of military activities in the Asian Pacific on United States-Japanese security needs. Second, there is no certainty that greater Japanese defense spending would help United States economic performance. Third, the argument implies that United States security concerns are totally inseparable from overall United States global security commitments. An increase in Japan's defense spending does not automatically guarantee a reduction in United States defense spending.

Summary

Since the Nakasone Administration, Japan has made solid strides in defense such that by 1988 its defense expenditures had slightly exceeded one percent of GNP. The trade issue currently generates a great deal of friction in the relationship between the United States and Japan. The frictions are enhanced partly by the reactions of an economic superpower in the process of losing its number one economic status. In part also, they are caused by Japan's almost exclusive focus on power economic capabilities. A new security relationship is steadily evolving characterized not by the patron (United States)-client (Japan) relationship of the 1980s but by a relationship of mutual security-dependence based on a partnership whose function is to maintain peace and stability in developing regions in particular.

Japan's obvious security importance is based on its economic superpower status and its importance to the West, and its increasing dynamism in the area of advanced high technology components relevant to United States weapons systems. If the trend of United States relative economic decline continues, the United States could drift toward increased dependence on Japan in high-technological components in particular. Continued Japanese aid flows to strategic allies—the Philippines, Turkey or Egypt, among others—enhance United States security objectives. An increasing Japanese independent posture away from United States cooperation, on the other hand, could mean increased cooperation with a not so friendly power to the United States. Besides, the threat of nuclear proliferation now appears more threatening due largely to the disintegration of the Soviet Union. However, the security climate and other aspects of the international landscape point toward increased linkage of defense burden sharing and economic interactions. Global change and relative United States decline all enhance the pressures for increased Japanese global involvement and power projection in cooperation with United States global concerns.

The American pressure on Japan for increased burden sharing conveys the impression that it is trying to get Japan to be its proxy, or at least its economic proxy. The trend is actually a reversal of reality because the United States has been Japan's proxy for so long that many are surprised that Japan has been allowed to indulge in free riding for so long. Mutual security-dependence involves getting Japan to assume its fair share of burdens that are commensurate with its power economic capabilities. The current economic woes—massive debts and trade budget deficits—of the United States will increasingly compel the United States to reduce its global commitments, while increasing pressure will fall on Japan for security burden sharing commensurate with its economic power. At the same time Japan will continue to enhance its economic power while its domestic politics and regional realities will continue to constrain the military dimension of its comprehensive security. Japan still lacks a national consensus as to the extent of diplomatic efforts it should undertake in pursuit of comprehensive security. There are some, for example, who still cling to the basic elements of the Yoshida posture. A posture named after Prime Minister Shigeru Yoshida (1946 and 1954) it called for Japan to refrain from maintaining a high profile on volatile and explosive international issues, and focus virtually all of the nation's energies on economic pursuits.

In addition, the convergence of four trends—the end of the Cold War, the demise of the Soviet Union, Japan's rapid ascent as an economic superpower, and the perceived relative economic decline of the United States—have brought into sharper focus the debate about Japan's current and future international role. Policy preferences with Japan regarding Japan's role in the world and its relationship with the United States are many and include: isolationism especially in relation to military security issues, autonomy in relation to interactions with the United States, increased internationalism to reflect its economic power, and stronger bilateral relations and cooperation with the United States, among others. The issue of military internationalism is one that would long be plagued by doubts, dilemmas, and indecision as Japan's unhindered economic globalism gets entangled in explosive regional situations in the Middle East and other regions, as Japan experiences increased pressures from the United States and other allies for more defense burden sharing and direct involvement in collective security efforts, and as Japan sees the need to take more independent action related to its own territorial defense.

Endnotes

1 See, for example, Richard H. Ullman, "Redefining Security," *International Security* 8 (Summer 1983), pp. 129-153; Kal J. Holsti, "Politics in Command: Foreign Trade as National Security Policy," *International Organization* 40 (Summer 1986), pp. 643-671; and Arthur H. Westing, "An Expanded Concept of International Security," *Global Resources and International Conflict: Environmental Factors in Strategic Policy and Action* (New York: Oxford University Press, 1986) pp. 183-200.

2 See, "Discriminate Deterrence," a paper by the Regional Conflict Working Group submitted to the *Commission on Integrated Long-Term Strategy* (Washington, D.C.: Government Printing Office, May 1988).

3 See, for example, *Speaking of Japan*, Vol. 9 No. 96, December 1988, pp. 20-24.

4 For further details, see, William Howard Taft IV, U.S. Deputy Secretary of Defense, "Burden Sharing, Japan's Contribution to Collective Security," speech delivered at the National Press Club, Tokyo, May 12, 1988, in *Speaking of Japan*, vol. 9, No. 92, August 1988, pp. 18-21.

5 *Speaking of Japan*, Vol. 9, No. 96, December 1988, p. 20.

6 For detailed discussions of these security concerns in Japan's foreign policy, see, Tsuneo Akaha, "Japanese Security Policy after U.S. Hegemony," *Millennium*, Vol. 18, no. 3 (Winter 1989) pp. 435-454; and Yoichi Funabashi, *Keizai anzenhosho: Chikyukeizai jidai no pawa ekonomikkusu* (Power economics in the age of global economy) Tokyo: Tokyokeizai shimposha, 1978.

7 For more on this, see Gregg Rubinstein, "U.S.-Japan Security Relations," *The Fletcher Forum*, Vol. 12, No. 1, (Winter 1988) p. 43.

8 *JEI Report*, No. 19A (by Barbara Wanner) May 13, 1988, p.6.

9 Edward A. Olsen, *U.S.-Japan strategic reciprocity: A neo-nationalist view* (Stanford, Calif: Hoover Institution Press, 1985) p. 106.

10 For an extensive examination of the concept, see Tsuneo Akada, "Comprehensive Security as an Alternative to Military Security in the Post-Hegemonic World: The Japanese Model and its Applicability in East Asia," paper presented at the annual convention of the International Studies Association, Washington, D.C., April 10-14, 1990; and "Japanese Comprehensive Security Policy: The Maritime Dimension," paper presented at the annual convention of the International Studies Association, Anaheim, California, March 25-29, 1986.

11 See, Robert W. Barnett, *Beyond War: Japan's Concept of Comprehensive National Security* (Washington, D.C.: Pergamon-Brasseys, 1984).

12 See, for example, Joseph A. Grimes, "Interdependence and Self-Interest, Defining Japan's Global Role," speech delivered May 7, 1988, *Speaking of Japan* Vol. 9, No. 92, August 1988, pp. 6–11.

13 See Saburo Okita, "Sustainable Internationalism: A Multilateral approach to Economic Revitalization," speech delivered at the Yomiuri Symposium on the International Economy '88, May 12, 1988, *Speaking of Japan* Vol. 9, No. 93, September 1988, pp. 6–11.

14 For facts and figures on the Japanese debates and discussions, see, "Japan Restricted in Ways to Help, Will Send Medical Aid to Middle East," *Washington Post*, August 24, 1990; "Kaifu Outlines His Proposal for Unarmed Japanese in Gulf," *New York Times*, September 28, 1990; "The Mouse That Was Stillborn," *Economist* November 10, 1990, pp. 36–38; and "Japan Stares Down the Barrel of a Gun," *Economist*, February 2, 1991, pp. 31–32.

15 For further details, see, Tsuneo Akaha, "Comprehensive Security as an Alternative to Military Security in the Post-Hegemonic World: The Japanese Model and its Applicability in East Asia," paper presented at the annual convention of the International Studies Association, Washington, D.C., April 10–14, 1990.

16 These principles were part of Prime Minister Takeshita's speech, "A Nation Contributing More to the World: Japan's Commitment to Global Prosperity," speech delivered at the National Press Club in Washington on January 14, 1988, *Speaking of Japan*, Vol. 9, No. 89 (May 1988) pp. 27–32.

17 See Ministry of Foreign Affairs, "International Cooperation Initiative (Contributing to the Peace and Prosperity of the World," January 1989).

18 See, again, Ministry of Foreign Affairs, "International Cooperation Initiative (Contributing to the Peace and Prosperity of the World," January 1989).

19 For further details, see, *U.S. Overseas Loans and Grants and Assistance from International Organization*, 1990 (Washington, D.C.: Government Printing Office, 1991).

20 See, for example, George R. Packard, "New Directions, Changes in Japan's Self-Image and Global Role," *Speaking of Japan* Vol. 9, No. 90, June 1988, pp. 6–15.

21 For further details, see, *JEI Report*, No. 6B (by Susan Macknight) February 12, 1988, pp. 8–10.

22 *Japan Economic Survey: A Monthly Review of U.S.-Japan Economic Relations*, Vol. XII, No. 9, September 1988, pp. 5 and 12.

23 *JEI Report*, No. 19A (by Barbara Wanner) May 13, 1988, p.2.

24 Foreign Broadcast Information Service (FBIS) Daily Report, Dec. 31, 1983: C10.

25 *Washington Post*, Dec. 4, 1982, p. 1; and FBIS 4 (Jan. 25, 1983: C7).

6

HEGEMONIC STABILITY THEORY AND THE
UNITED STATES-JAPAN RELATIONSHIP

The introduction of the hegemonic stability theory in the early 1970s marked the beginning of the application of various analyses to international economic relations, especially the structure of trade among advanced industrial countries. The theory has since been modified, reinterpreted, and given added importance because of its relevance to the profound shocks in the global economic system in the 1970s, and its major premise of a significant decline in United States hegemonic leadership.[1] The main objective of this chapter is to apply the different variants of hegemonic stability theory to U.S.-Japan economic interactions especially as they relate to the postwar free trade environment. The principal hypothesis of hegemonic stability theory, which argues that the presence of a strong hegemonic state in the international system is necessary for its stability, is examined in relation to U.S.-Japan economic cooperation and/or conflicts, and shifts in the concentration of economic power between them from the 1950s to the present. The main focus of the analysis is to find out whether, and to what degree, shifts in the concentration of economic power has dynamic effects on U.S.-Japan cooperative or conflictual interactions to change policies. Is freer trade largely attributable to the effectiveness of U.S. hegemonic leadership? Or is U.S. hegemonic decline accounting for increasing trade frictions? In sum, this chapter will: (1) briefly review the literature on the theory of hegemonic stability and underscore its relevance to U.S.-Japan interactions; (2) examine U.S.-Japan cooperative and conflictual behavior in aid, trade and investment activities; and (3) analyze the most recent U.S. hegemonic role, and Japan's supportive role, in the Persian Gulf War.

Hegemonic Stability Theory: A Brief Review of the Literature

Current applications of hegemony have focused primarily at the level of international relations to explore, for example, the conception of a "hegemonic world order" in the light of changes in the configurations of power and influence in the global system. In the view of Robert W. Cox, for example, to be hegemonic:

> a state would have to found and protect a world order that was universal in conception, i.e., not an order directly expressing the interest of one state but an order that most states could find compatible with their interests given their different levels of power and lesser abilities to change that order. The less powerful states could live with the order even if they could not change it.[2]

Hegemony, then, is maintained to the extent that international consent takes precedence over coercion. It is a temporal globalization in thought of a particular power structure within a *modus vivendi* conceived not as domination but as the necessary and natural order of things.

In hegemony, there is an implicit as well as an explicit configuration of factors that make one actor dominant in the international system. In the areas of efficiency, scope and salience of activities, and in sense of task this dominant power excels over others. This translates into a situation where it is the most efficient producer of goods in the international economy and commands the most efficient means of global military power projection. The scope of its interests and commitments overlaps with and is coterminous with most domestic, regional, and international issues; its salience stems from the pervasiveness of its economic and political influence such that no other actor in the system can afford to ignore it and that their international relations revolve around its behavior. It, in turn, feels responsible for maintaining a stable world order and thus articulates its responsibility in universal terms.

The consolidation of hegemony involves the interactive and reinforcing influence of condign power (threats and punitive actions), compensatory power (resource transfers to actors) and conditioned power (persuasion, appeal to belief).[3] In other words, maintaining hegemonic stability rests on the mutually reinforcing relationships of punitive, remunerative, and normative capabilities of the dominant power. The preeminent position of a hegemon is a consequence of war. It emerges from the war as the leading military and economic actor. In short, the hegemon occupies a leading position in the international hierarchy of power, wealth, and prestige.[4] This outcome guarantees order in the international system because other powers realize they are weaker in relative terms; no power is likely to challenge this international order by force. The situation of dominance in economic capabilities confers remunerative or compensatory advantages on the dominant power and complements its power politico-military capabilities for it enables it to transfer resources to allies and clients. It also allows it to produce quality civilian and military goods. In addition, the hegemonic power commands enhanced legitimacy through its normative capabilities. It is capable of pointing to its values, ideology, and entire way of life as a source of emulation for other actors.

If hegemonic consolidation is a process in which condign, compensatory, and conditioned capabilities are mutually reinforcing, then hegemonic decline, on the other hand, may be viewed as a process of mutually reinforcing decline of these same capabilities. This "vicious circle" affects relationships with other powers and in turn affects the nature of the international system. In a word, it transforms it from a hegemonic system to a balance-of-power system. Gilpin considers high relative productivity to be a necessary precondition for the maintenance of global predominance. To be a hegemon, in other words, entails costs and responsibilities—maintenance of a superior military, financial support for allies, foreign aid and sacrifices associated with maintaining a global economy. Gilpin argues that to meet these costs requires the continuing production of economic surplus, because they (the costs) "are not productive investments; they constitute an economic drain on the economy of the dominant state."[5] In terms of the global economy, a high relative productivity guarantees this economic surplus.

Gilpin then goes on to discuss that the economic surplus is directed into the three basic functions of consumption, production and protection. Consumption includes public and private consumption of the goods and services of the dominant state. Production or productive investment refers to that part of a territorial state's economy that is reinvested into the productive sector to increase the productivity of land, labor and capital. Protection relates to the costs of protecting the "national interest"—safe-guarding national security, maintenance of military forces, financing allies, weapons production, and the like.

Hegemonic stability theory is predicated on the claim that the global system tends towards stability—conditions conducive to the optimal provision of international public goods—as long as it is dominated by a hegemon (a single and overwhelmingly preponderant nation). A significant decline in the hegemonic status of the hegemon manifested in its increasing inability to influence the outcomes of international interactions would account directly for the increased instability—that is a general antipathy towards bearing the cost of international public goods. Such antipathy could be manifested in neomercantilist behavior, or increased use of state intervention to contain declining global competitiveness. The concentration of economic power, in other words, becomes a direct and strong determinant of systemic stability—that is, the successful operation of the international market in general and on the supply of international public goods in particular. Hegemonic stability theory, compared to other theories of international relations such as the balance of power, imperialism and dependency, commands great appeal. Hegemonic stability theory conveys the idea of a benign hegemon preoccupied with international systemic stability thereby ensuring conditions conducive to the optimal provision of international public goods beneficial to even the weakest state.[6] In hegemonic stability theory, it is strongly implied that nation-states, though they struggle for power relative to each other, also desire and achieve cooperation even if involuntarily.

Hegemonic decline is predicated on the argument that changing structural characteristics of the international system will contribute to the weakening of the hegemon over time. Declining power will create pressures for the hegemonic power to adjust its policies to contain the new situational context. Containing the new situation involves adoption of policies which will slow down the process of decline and account for the cost of defending the hegemonic order. Accordingly, we should expect the hegemon as a declining power to forego peripheral commitments abroad and adjust policies to expand resources internally. Containing a declining situational context for the hegemon is predicated on the obvious logic that failure to adjust old policies will result in a pattern of escalating costs and declining benefits.

The United States-Japan Relationship in the Context of Hegemony

That inequality contributes to order in international relations, has become an axiom of hegemonic stability theory. However, when the hegemon progressively experiences a loss in power and wealth, a situation of relative equality develops among key international state actors. The system in this sense becomes less hegemonic, less orderly and slips into a balance of power pattern of interaction.[7]

World War II transformed the American economy into a superpower economy that controlled roughly 50 percent of the Gross World Product. This predominant economic position inevitably thrust the U.S. into the role of helping to rebuild the devastated economies of the West European countries and Japan. Japan, one of the countries rebuilt under U.S. auspices and U.S. capital soon recovered and with other countries became a challenge to the U.S. because their growth rates surpassed those of the U.S.. Between 1953 and 1960, the average growth rate for America's GDP was 2.4 percent; the growth rate for Japan was 9.4 percent, Japan being exempted from military expenditures. Between 1950 and 1976 the average growth in industrial productivity for the U.S. and Japan were 2.8 percent and 8.3 percent respectively.[8] In the 1950s, that is, the greater productivity of other nations, began to rival the competitiveness of American industries. Starting with 1955 the U.S. experienced its first negative trade balance in the area of textiles and manufactured consumer durables. Other negative trade balances occurred in 1959 in consumer goods, 1962 in electric household appliances and radios, iron and steel in 1963 and automotive products in 1968.[9]

The relative decline of the U.S. economy can be seen in proper perspective when compared to the relative surge of the Japanese economy. The contrast between the two is found in the area of trade in particular. In 1985, when the American trade deficit reached $117.7 billion, Japan was grappling with a trade surplus with the U.S. of close to $50 billion. According to the *New York Times* (1984) the biggest share of U.S. imports during this time was with Japan.[10] Items imported were mostly data processing equipment, automobile parts, transistors and semiconductors, and telecommunications equipment, among others. Throughout the 1980s in general, the U.S. economy experienced unprecedented trade deficits every new year. From 1982 the annual deficit grew from $42.7 billion to over $100 billion in 1984.

Impacting on these conditions of relative declining productivity, has been the U.S. involvement in substantial military spending. While the size of military allocations may not be remarkable, the length of the spending pattern is significant. Military spending has been consistent since the end of World War II and the end of the Reagan era. Between 1979 and 1986, military expenditures increased by an average of 8 percent per annum. In 1979 and 1980 President Carter spent roughly $200 billion a year on the military. In 1986 President Reagan spent nearly $300 billion.[11]

As the former East-West divisions give way to new issues, concerns and views about the growing status and influence of Japan loom large. The U.S. and Europe, in particular, have widely different views of Japan's ability to prosper and dominate. According to a July 1990 Business Week/NHK/Harris Poll, 30 percent of Europeans and 18 percent of Americans expect Japan to become the world's leading economic power by the end of the century. There was strong agreement among respondents about the grim outlook for the U.S. role in the world economy. Asked about the U.S. share of the world market in 10 years, 73 percent of Japanese, 54 percent of European, and 47 percent of American respondents said it would decrease. Growth in the U.S. has already slipped below 2 percent. Higher oil prices are expected to add 14.5 billion on to the U.S. trade deficit.[12]

Iraq's threat in the Persian Gulf allied the industrialized nations in a way that has not been seen since the oil shocks of the 1970s. In the Gulf Crisis, the relationship between the U.S., Western Europe, and Japan was one of "positive cooperation" because of their shared or congruent values regarding stability in the Middle East and uninterrupted access to oil. Under normal conditions and based on U.S. relative economic decline, the U.S. relationship with Japan progressively becomes one of "adversarial cooperation" in reference to the common interests of competitors irrespective of value incongruence. This is cooperation based on, or regardless of, conflicting goals, in recognition that the alternatives to cooperation might be too costly to pursue. The U.S. and Japan, for example, have bargained over their trade frictions and economic behavior in order to control the costs and limit the risks of conflict and to manage their most fundamental mutual economic interest: the avoidance of trade war. The U.S.-Japan relationship is akin to what Schelling noted in his *The Strategy of Conflict*, rivals "may just be in the same boat together—" this means that, whatever else they do, they have a shared interest "in not tipping the boat."[13] Such cooperative behavior in fact becomes an ongoing process aimed at seeking more preferred outcomes because certain goals may be put off until conditions change. For example, the U.S. and Japan each might prefer balance of trade surplus over the other as the preferred outcome for their respective economies, but the policies and postures of each make maintaining a permanent trade surplus position impossible or too adversarial to achieve. The need to manage the "adversarial" relationship and maintain "acceptable symmetry" in the continuing transactions may encourage ongoing cooperative behavior.

It could be argued that the U.S. and Japan are in the process of developing a separate trade *regime* governing their economic relationship, and based largely on this competitive kind of cooperation. It may be that the cumulative experience has helped produce conditions that will permit and may even promote more "positive cooperation" in the future. Cooperation between the U.S. and Japan is, of course, obvious in many ways. Certainly, the prevailing view since the 1970s is that the U.S.-Japan economic relationship has involved many areas of friction that have produced many instances of agreements and overall cooperation on substantive matters, especially so with regard to their economic interests. The clash of economic tactics and interests is usually followed by a period of negotiations, bargaining, and concessions aimed at yielding acceptable outcomes even if they are not the most preferred ones.

The notion of regime, or the regime concept may help clarify the meaning, role and significance of cooperative behavior between the U.S. and Japan. The focus of analysis here is: does the regime concept facilitate our understanding of the dynamics of international economic relationship? In particular, is it relevant and useful to describe and explain the economic relationship between the U.S. and Japan in regime terms? In the U.S.-Japan relationship, both nations belong to real world regimes such as GATT or the IMF, and they are also bound by the more amorphous "rules of the game" that constrain their behavior in various issue areas, such as—in the case of this analysis—economic relations. A number of consensus definitions of regime exist in this literature, such as that of Stephen Krasner:

> Regimes can be defined as sets of implicit or explicit principles, norms, rules, or decision-making procedures around which actors' expectations converge in a given area of international relations. Principles are beliefs of fact, causation, and rectitude. Norms are standards of behavior defined in terms of rights and obligations. Rules are specific prescriptions or proscriptions for action. Decision-making procedures are prevailing practices for making and implementing collective choice.[14]

Even when such norms or principles bind relations between states, often they have to cooperate in reminding one another of their existence, or fill in the gaps where they do not cover unforeseen conflictual situations. This means that a regime is an idealized system. It may conform closely to the real world or depart from it considerably. Cooperation facilitates its application and enhances its relevance to the interacting entities.

Relative U.S. economic decline linked to Japan's dramatic economic recovery and expansion contributed largely to the "adversarial" cooperation "regime" to develop. Trade frictions, in particular, placed the U.S. and Japan in the same boat, that of mutual, unavoidable, systemic vulnerability. They have chosen a more rational way to solve their mutual situation: they have realized the full implications of their shared risks and have therefore embarked on a series of collaboration ventures to manage the relationship in recognition of their mutual economic interest.

The principles and understandings, rules, and rights and obligations that have already been established in the U.S.-Japan relationship can be summarized as follows: (1) recognition of trade symmetry and "parity" of the two nations and their continuous efforts to create a more favorable economic climate between them as the first and third largest economic units in the world. In this relationship, mutual economic vulnerability is the motor of cooperation, whether the two like it or not. Economic superpower status also enters into this consideration of symmetry. Both sides thus treat this relationship of symmetry as a condition which both are obligated to recognize and maintain. Moreover, it appears to be a basic condition for cooperation in other matters. Without recognition of "equal status" and symmetry, most of the mutual concerns will begin to disappear. (2) Interaction based on a high level of technological cooperation. In more recent years the U.S.-Japan technological cooperation has been strengthening. In June 1990, the U.S. asked Japan to invest $2 billion and take a leading management role in the building of a giant superconducting supercollider in Texas. It would constitute the largest scientific collaboration between the two countries. Other joint technological projects of importance include the FSX project designed at upgrading Japan's military defenses, and the $30 billion space station. (3) An institutionalized economic negotiation process to maintain the regime and relationship. This process is especially seen in the sector by sector negotiations in areas like semiconductors, textiles, automobiles, beef, and citrus products. Second, are the U.S.-Japanese talks aimed at the structural impediments to trade, known as Structural Impediments Initiative (SII) talks. Their focus is on how each country manages its economy, organizes its business, and sets basic priorities for its people; all macroeconomic policies that may not be intentional barriers to trade but still hinder U.S. competitiveness in Japan. (4) Economic cooperation to support economic stability and prosperity in Third World regions. It is now the view among top officials in the Japan foreign aid program, that Japan can more effectively promote its own national interests by promoting the interests of other countries—both developed and developing. As now the world's largest creditor and the fact of its growing economic power projection, it is also in the process of relieving part of the security burden on the U.S. by picking up some of the slack created by the dwindling U.S. aid budget since the early 1980s. Japan's foreign aid has been targeted mostly at strategically-located, moderate countries like Egypt, Pakistan, Turkey, Jordan, Yemen, and Sudan. In 1986 Egypt was the tenth largest recipient of Japan's ODA totalling $126 million.[15] While Tokyo does not extend military aid, it nonetheless increased economic aid to countries that are strategic to the Western alliance.

Culture Conflict and Cooperative U.S.-Japan Interactions

The cultural differences between the U.S. and Japan largely underlie the existing trade frictions between the two countries. The dynamics of the way Japanese conduct business is frustrating to the expectations of American business *modus operandi*. The *keiretsu*, the existence of an almost impenetrable set of alliances of financial and personal ties that bind Japanese subcontractor to manufacturer to wholesaler to retailer, constitutes one of the most formidable challenges for the United States. It is an integral part of Japan's indigenous and exclusive business culture that the government itself considers hard to regulate. It is no longer the legal barriers—quotas, excessive tariffs—that frustrate the foreigner, because these have been resolved through negotiations, but it is the *keiretsu*. This alliance of Japan's most powerful firms (Mitsui, Mitsubishi, Sumitomo, Fuji etc.) through interlocking holdings owns over 70 percent of shares on Japan's stock markets. Lesser versions of the industrial combines, or *Zaibatsu*, of wartime Japan, the *keiretsu* enable rival manufacturers to fix prices and divide markets among themselves. In the U.S. and Europe such activities would be illegal under antitrust laws but in Japan they provoke only mild government warnings. The consequence is that many commodity items (cars and electronic items) are based on exclusive dealerships and affiliations.

Another aspect of Japan's economic strategy against foreign goods is the fact that only Japanese goods carry the guarantee of being returned to the wholesaler if they fail to sell. Imports do not. More Japanese retailers are thus kept in business than even in the U.S. (1.6 million versus 1.4 million in 1989).[16] A consequence of this economic defense of the Japanese retailers is that they end up charging the world's highest prices, even on items considered basic like food, wine, cosmetics, bed linens, and so on.

Based on the above example and others, some critics of Japanese international economic trading behavior argue that Japanese economic life is fundamentally different from that of other advanced industrial nations, especially the U.S.. Japan is viewed as a production-oriented and not a consumption-oriented society. The government is said to be export promotion oriented but suppresses domestic consumption. Among other things, import restraints are built into the culture—too ingrained to be eliminated through trade negotiations. This view of Japan has prompted some Americans to suggest that Japan should be "contained," like the former Soviet Union. They call for unilateral American action to reduce the trade gap.

On the Japanese side, there are indications that the Japanese are increasingly expressing feelings of independence sometimes bordering on disgust for the United States. In their book, Sony Corporation founder Akio Morita and Shintaro Ishihara, a novelist and far right-wing Diet member of Japan's ruling Liberal Democratic Party, characterized the U.S.-Japanese relationship as a "fatal attraction." They further referred to the U.S. as a "shifty country" that should start playing more by Japanese rules if it does not want Tokyo to stop selling it the microchips essential for targeting U.S. missiles and begin selling them to the Soviets.[17] The commentary on microchips reflects Japanese technological dominance in the U.S.-Japanese relationship, whereas the comments on the U.S. as a shifty nation express views aired and common in Japan for a long time. The statements in the book signal a strong current of reduced Japanese dependence on the United States. It could be interpreted as a growing assertion by the Japanese that the era of total Japanese dependence is gone and should now be replaced by a relationship of mutual power dependence, a manifestation of the relative decline in U.S. hegemony.

The U.S.-Japan bilateral relationship while plagued by a gigantic cultural chasm has nevertheless produced immense advantages to both sides. For the U.S., Japan constituted a central sphere of operation in the superpower military and political rivalry with the former U.S.S.R. in the Far East. For Japan the benefit has come in the form of economic power—trade and investments—and military security without having to shoulder most of the defense burden. The U.S.-Japan relationship is now more likely destined to change. The demise of the Soviet Union has given Americans less reason to fear the nuclear and communist threat that dominated world politics for the last forty years. With the old threat virtually gone, attention is being progressively focused on the incompatibilities in the U.S.-Japan relationship, such that Americans are increasingly identifying the new threat to American security to be Japan. Recent polls are evidence of the American shift in attitude. The consequence is that the bilateral relationship is increasingly being politicized even as the two huge economies are still so pervasively interdependent.

The cultural conflicts intermesh with cooperative efforts in aid, trade and investment issues. In June 1990, the U.S.-Japanese technological cooperation received a new boost when the U.S. asked Japan to invest $2 billion and take a leading management role in the building of a giant superconducting supercollider in Texas. It would constitute the largest scientific collaboration between the two countries. Scientific and technological cooperation between the two countries is not without its critics in both countries. In the U.S., American corporate executives and members of Congress complain that Japan has acted as a sponge for technologies developed in the United States, while it contributes relatively little basic research of its own. In Japan, critics accuse the U.S. of seeking Japan's help only when it is engaging in projects it cannot afford on its own. Critics further resent America for excluding Japan from some American projects like computer chips, or relegating Japan to a junior role in projects like the proposed $30 billion space station.[18]

In the early part of 1990, Washington and Tokyo engaged in a range of negotiations on various issues to reduce the American trade deficit with Japan which has remained at about $50 billion since the mid 1980s and has become the focus of rising economic tensions. In February 1990, shortly after the governing LDPs election victory, President Bush called on Prime Minister Kaifu to take further action in the trade area. This persuasive action came shortly after the conclusion of the latest round of "structural impediments" talks with Japan which involved pressure on Japan to agree to several basic changes in the way business is conducted in Japan in order to ease the way for increased imports. The action by President Bush was an indication of American disappointment with what seemed to be Japanese resistance to American requests.

In the trade issue, rocked by serious contention, the U.S. in putting pressure on Japan to spend more for public works, weaken the influence of the *keiretsu* (powerful Japanese cartels), and relax laws that allow small retailers to block large stores from operating in their neighborhoods. The steps taken by Japan in this area have so far not yet given American exporters more access to Japanese markets. The Japanese, on the other hand, are also exercising pressure on the U.S. to take its own steps. They are requesting for the U.S. to reduce the federal deficit, increase domestic savings and implement corporate reforms that would place greater emphasis on long-term growth, education, research and development so that the American ability to compete would improve. In other words, according to Japan, the trade deficit is caused more by American economic shortcomings than by Japanese economic barriers.

In June 1990, a year after tough negotiations on a series of social and economic reforms, both countries reached agreement on ways to reduce the huge U.S. bilateral trade deficit and change the way the two countries do business. The reforms are measures to remove structural impediments to trade which specify among other things that the U.S. will reduce its federal debt and budget deficit and that Japan will significantly increase spending on public works and strictly enforce antitrust laws. According to economic theory, expenditure on public works projects increases domestic demand and attracts more imports.

The agreements are supposed to serve as a deterrent against protectionist moves in Congress. According to the Japanese, they will substantially contribute to improving the Japanese standard of living while also creating more harmony between the Japanese economy and the world economy. The key positions of the trade agreement are presented in Table 6.1. Such negotiations reflect elements of competitive cooperation, culture incompatibilities, and hegemonic management, and mutual power-dependence. The outcome of the negotiations in fact reveal a new assertiveness by Japan.

Japan, for example, refused to give in to the American request that Japan increase its level of public works spending to $3.3 trillion (500 trillion yen) during the next ten years.[19] The Japanese nonetheless promised far-reaching reforms such as giving more authority to the Fair Trade Commission. But Japan also refused to introduce new categories of trade complaints as the U.S. had wanted. The two sides promised to hold regular meetings to review implementation of the reforms agreed upon so far.

Table 6.1

United States-Japan Economic Agreements

United States	*Japan*
1. Cut the federal budget deficit and reduce government debt	Increase spending on public works to $2.77 trillion in the 1991–2000 decade
2. Stimulate private savings and investment by creating family savings accounts, enhancing existing individual retirement accounts and cutting capital gains tax	Reduce from three days to one the time it takes for imports to clear customs
3. Revise laws to allow for new joint ventures, limit product liability awards and stimulate investment in new plant equipment and research and development	Crackdown on bid-rigging, price-setting, oligopolistic behavior and coercive business practices that limit competition
4. Improve education and job training programs	Revise land policy to tame skyrocketing real estate prices
5.	Amend regulations to liberalize trucking, retailing and pharmaceuticals industries
6.	Improve patent protection for foreign companies.

Source: A *Los Angeles Times* Report; *Tampa Tribune*, Friday, June 29, 1990, p. 2-A.

Managing Hegemony: Positive Cooperation in the Persian Gulf War

The theory of hegemonic stability is also based on the understanding that the hegemon and its allies will contain new and threatening situations to stability by adjusting their policies and implementing strategies which will strengthen the status quo and account for the cost of defending the hegemonic order. When it comes to the military aspect of hegemony, the U.S. has unrivaled dominance in the Western alliance, but when it comes to socio-economic matters the U.S. often has to negotiate, and urge Europe or Japan to make concessions. The recent U.S. role in the Gulf War is an example of U.S. military superiority even in the face of alleged "hegemonic decline." The decline is partly manifested in its pressure on Japan and other allies to engage in burden sharing to restore balance in the Persian Gulf. The increasing pressure on allies, who are also economic competitors, to share the burdens of leadership is a manifestation of the fact that the U.S. has been gradually losing its ability to pursue goals above and beyond those basic interests imposed by the global system. Ordinarily, a hegemonic state is so powerful that its primary interests can be adequately secured using only a portion of its multidimensional resources.

As the international system becomes threatened by events like the 1973 Arab oil embargo, the Iran-Iraq War, and the 1991 Gulf War, the nature of Japanese pacifism and dependence on U.S. military protection is increasingly put to the test. The Gulf crisis was so integral to Japan's national interest that it was perceived as some sort of state of emergency. The Middle East region is the source of almost 70 percent of Japan's crude oil supplies. In security terms, the region is therefore of strategic importance to Japan. Its real and potential dilemmas in the region have impelled it to utilize foreign aid as a central vehicle in efforts to promote stability in the region. This, coupled with its hegemonic cooperation with the U.S. and other Western powers, made Japan decide, among other things, to extend an additional $9 billion in monetary cooperation to the U.S.-led multinational force by the end of the 1990/1991 fiscal year. Japan also expressed willingness to dispatch Self-Defense Forces (SDF) aircraft to the Gulf for the evacuation of afflicted refugees.

Japan's contribution to the Gulf War effort were indicative of Japan's political and economic stake in the conflict as an ally of the Western alliance and in terms of its dependence on the U.S. military security umbrella. Japan is being so rapidly propelled into the maelstrom of world politics in general and the Gulf crisis in particular that, some argue, its decision to dispatch SDF planes to the Gulf was unconstitutional. It, in fact, moved to modify a government ordinance to legitimize the dispatch of the planes and bring its action in line with the peace principle of the constitution.

In the area of defense buildup, Japan is impelled toward an upward momentum in spending because of: (1) U.S. Congressional urgings for Japan to spend more to make U.S. defense reductions possible; and (2) the perceived threat posed by the Soviet forces in Northeast Asia. In 1989 President Bush signed a defense bill that urged Japan to increase its military expenditure and required the U.S. to negotiate an agreement for Japan to completely offset the costs of maintaining the 50,000 American service personnel stationed there. Currently, 45 percent (about $2.8 billion) of the annual expenses for the Americans in Japan is shouldered by Japan. Critics in the U.S. argue that the ceiling (now slightly over 1 percent) that Japan imposed on its defense outlays is roughly equal to those of Britain, Germany, or France.[20] Japan also develops state-of-the art military technology for its defense. The defense expenditure increases have contributed to the creation of a sophisticated anti-submarine network in straits in the Northwest Pacific. This is also backed up by a sophisticated number of advanced fighter jets estimated at 300 now.

The assembling of a multinational force of 28 nations with the active cooperation of Britain, France, Italy, and Japan is exemplary of cooperation during a period of U.S. relative economic decline. After World War II, "the United States constructed a liberal-capitalist world political economy based on multilateral principles and embodying rules that the United States approved."[21] The U.S. has since made tremendous efforts to reduce tariffs and other barriers to trade often at its own expense. In monetary relations, for example, the U.S. actively worked to provide sufficient international liquidity for the conduct of free trade. In its efforts to maintain its hegemony the U.S. often permitted Europe to discriminate against its exports; it also ran a persistent balance of payments deficit in the interest of promoting a prosperous and stable world economy.

The U.S. has also since used its extensive capabilities to guarantee for itself and its allies "secure and reasonably priced access to oil from the Middle East"—a key factor for the astonishing economic growth and widespread global economic transactions experienced after 1945. The recent American response to Iraq's threat to uninterrupted oil flow is a manifestation of American hegemony in oil which, according to Keohane rests among other things, on (1) strong political ties with the conservative Arab regimes; (2) the transfer of military and technical aid to many oil-producing countries; and (3) the capacity to intervene in the domestic politics of the Middle East.[22] The oil dimension of American hegemony is so crucial to its overall hegemony that the U.S. established a formal international regime in oil in November 1974 following the disastrous events of 1973 and 1974.[23] Again the U.S. was able in February of 1974 to convene a meeting of 13 major oil-consuming states in Washington. A communique issued at the conclusion of the Washington Energy Conference called "for a comprehensive action program to deal with all facets of the world energy situation by cooperative measures."[24] Many of the nations that participated in the multinational force in the Persian Gulf were present at the conference creating the International Energy Agency (IEA). They included: Belgium, Canada, Denmark, France, West Germany, Ireland, Italy, Japan, Luxembourg, the Netherlands, Norway, the U.K., and the United States.

The leadership role of the U.S. in the Persian Gulf crisis is indicative of a hegemonic leader, even though its role may seem to be more of that of a *primus inter pares*. In their Gulf War participation, the allied powers were either hegemonically-led and/or independently cooperative. Had their various political and economic interests not been at odds with Iraq's territorial ambitious, one might expect the industrialized powers of the allied group to have stopped short of participating in the war against Iraq. What we saw instead was solidarity among all major Middle Eastern oil consumers. An effective cooperation took place between the threatened conservative oil monarchies—Saudi Arabia, Oman, Quatar, and the Emirates—and the major oil-dependent industrialized countries, all adopted a collective-interest approach to the Iraqi threat.

Precisely because they apprehended the significance of oil for their economies, the industrialized states pursued cooperation instead to embrace a multilateral policy—going to war—designed to provide all of them a secure source of oil by removing the perceived threat of uninterrupted flow of Middle Eastern oil and threat to military security as well. Britain, France, Germany, Japan, Italy, and Holland, among other industrialized countries were all involved in one way or the other in the Gulf War. In terms of European cooperation with the U.S., the Gulf War stands in stark contrast to previous crises in which the U.S. has been involved. In the Iranian hostage crisis, the European allies refused to impose an embargo on Iran even though the U.S. had called upon them to do so. In the Soviet invasion of Afghanistan and the 1973 Yom Kippur War, among other events, the European nations adopted an approach contrary to U.S. wishes.

During the 1973 Arab oil embargo, the EC adopted a pro-Arab resolution in November 1973 on the Middle East. Later, Japan denounced Israeli policy with regard to the Palestinians. Moreover, each European state ignored a standing American offer of private exchanges on energy cooperation, while all distanced themselves from the conduct of American Middle East policy. However, after a great deal of ambivalence and vigorous unilateralism, each of the European states and Japan gave in to U.S. demand to form an oil consumer's regime.[25]

How else was the cooperation seen at the 1991 Gulf crisis explicable? This rather spontaneous collective action by the industrialized countries is like building on the foundation of the 1974 International Energy Agency regime between Europe, North America and Japan. In 1973 Henry Kissinger and President Nixon had to exert pressure upon the Europeans and Japan to secure their cooperation. In Kissinger's "Pilgrim Speech" of December 12, 1973, he proposed in London "that the nations of Europe, North America and Japan establish an Energy Action Group—with a mandate to develop within three months an initial program for collaboration in all areas of the energy problem."[26]

In the Middle East, as far as the industrialized nations are concerned, security and economic considerations are inevitably linked and access to oil is often going to be the trigger for collective Western action. What occurred in the Persian Gulf is reminiscent of the circumstances surrounding the Washington Energy Conference of 1974 when President Nixon stated:

> I believe that the, let me put it, the "enlightened selfish interest" of each nation here is better served by cooperation in trade, and by cooperation in developing our sources of energy and in acquiring the energy we need to keep the great industrial complex of the free world moving ahead to ever and ever higher plateaus.[27]

In the Gulf crisis, as in 1973–74, it seems obvious that American hegemonic leadership is essential for the cooperation of the advanced industrial states and Middle Eastern states threatened by Iraq's foreign policy objectives.

In the Gulf crisis, there was the American willingness to bear the burden of leadership, facilitated by its overwhelming military power. Critics would say that although U.S. trade and monetary assets have eroded substantially, potent American military power could still be instrumental in providing leadership and securing the cooperation of both industrialized and nonindustrialized countries.

Finally, the U.S.-Japan economic relationship and the 1991 U.S. role in the Gulf crisis is consistent with this view of hegemony:

1. Hegemonic tendencies are clearly identified mostly when crisis situations develop that threaten hegemonic stability. This is usually when the "carrot" and "stick" tactics are employed to bring about cooperation among allies and compliance among other states. In other words, success at restoring hegemonic stability, to a large extent, hinges upon the complementarity of interests among states. In the 1991 Gulf Crisis, the U.S. willingness to supply the greatest amount of military force to oust Iraq out of Kuwait was sufficient to nudge the other actors toward cooperation; the allied powers and others viewed a firm and decisive action against Iraq as the preferable strategy for ensuring regional stability and uninterrupted supply of oil. Above all, the recognition by Japan and Europe and the Middle Eastern states that such a military move would not be inimical to their interests was nonetheless a *sine qua non* for hegemonic cooperation.

2. Hegemony is not inseparable. The capabilities of a hegemon may vary by issue area. In the case of a hegemon whose power assets are in decline, assets in one issue area may be brought to bear to produce hegemonic outcomes in other issue areas. Thus, there is no necessary link between the erosion of a particular power asset and outcomes within the corresponding issue area. In the Persian Gulf crisis, the U.S. employed its overwhelming military superiority especially in technology to achieve a desired outcome in stability in the Middle East and security in oil flows.

Summary

This analysis of hegemonic stability theory and its relevance to the U.S.-Japan relationship suggests three implications. First, the major premise of hegemonic stability theory, that of a significant decline in U.S. hegemony, points to an evolving "adversarial cooperation" relationship because of the U.S. pressure to adjust its policies to slow down the process of decline and account for the cost of defending the hegemonic order. The ever-increasing U.S. negative trade balance, and the relative decline in the average growth in industrial productivity contrast sharply with the relative ascent of the Japanese economy, thereby resulting in economic frictions. Second, the constant economic frictions between the two nations, aggravated by culture incompatibilities and growing decline in U.S.

economic efficiency and salience of commercial activities, is producing a special economic *regime* between the two. The regime undoubtedly takes into account the fact that, first, Japanese economic life is fundamentally different from that of other advanced industrial countries. Second, that the U.S. needs to adjust its policies to decrease its federal budget deficit, stimulate private savings, among other things. The evolving regime is partly manifested in the super-301 section of the U.S. Omnibus Trade Act, or The Structural Impediments Initiative talks between the U.S. and Japan in particular. "The talks—are unprecedented: never in history have two superpowers delved so deeply into each other's domestic affairs."[28]

Third, the premise of a significant decline in U.S. hegemony implies a corresponding decrease in the remunerative economic capabilities of the U.S., prompting positive cooperation in the form of Japan, and others, supplying significant economic ("carrots") capabilities to effect hegemonic outcomes around the world. In the recent Gulf crisis, positive cooperation was seen at work. While the U.S. provided overwhelming military power ("sticks"), Japan and other industrialized countries supplied significant economic capabilities. In the end, the U.S. used its overwhelming military hegemony to effect an hegemonic out-come—the restoration of the status quo in the Persian Gulf. But with the demise of the Soviet Union, increasing relative U.S. economic decline, and continued Japanese economic ascent, the "adversarial" type of cooperation will come to underpin the U.S.-Japanese economic relationship.

Endnotes

1 Authors are divided in terms of whether American hegemony is still strong, has declined relatively, or has declined absolutely. Among those who argue that American hegemony is still strong in terms of the U.S. continued control over global outcomes are: Susan Strange, "Still an Extraordinary Power: America's Role in a Global Monetary System," in *Political Economy of International and Domestic Monetary Relations*, pp. 73–93, edited by Raymond E. Lombra and William Witte (Ames: Iowa State University Press, 1982); Bruce Russett, "The Mysterious Case of Vanishing Hegemony: Or is Mark Twain Really Dead?" *International Organization*, XXXIX 2 (Spring 1985), 207–234. In contrast, other theorists describe U.S. power in terms which suggests its absolute or relative decline. Robert O. Keohane, *After Hegemony: Cooperation and Discord in the World Political System* (Princeton: Princeton University Press, 1984); Richard Rosecrance, *America as an Ordinary Country* (Ithaca: Cornell University Press, 1976); Robert Gilpin, *U.S. Power and Multinational Corporation* (New York: Basic Books, 1975); and Paul Kennedy, *The Rise and Fall of the Great Powers* (New York: Random House, 1987).

2 Robert W. Cox, "Production and Hegemony: Toward a Political Economy of World Order," in Harold K. Jacobsen and Dusan Sidjanski (eds.), *The Emerging Industrial Economic Order* (Beverly Hills: Sage Publications, 1982) p. 45.

3 For more details on various dimensions of power, see, John K. Galbraith, *The Anatomy of Power* (Boston: Houghton Mifflin Company, 1983).

4 Robert Gilpin, *War and Change in World Politics*, (Cambridge: Cambridge University Press, 1981); and Ralph G. Hawtrey, *Economic Aspects of Sovereignty* (London: Longmans Green, 1952).

5 Robert Gilpin, *War and Change in World Politics*, p. 156f.

6 For more detailed discussions on the several appeals of the theory, see, Duncan Snidal, "The Limits of Hegemonic Stability" *International Organization* XXXIX 4 (Autumn 1985), p. 579.

7 See, for example, Robert Jervis (ed.), *International politics: Anarchy, force, political economy, and decision-making* (New York: Scott, Foresman, 1985).

8 Ricardo Parboni, *The Dollar and Its Rivals*, (London: New Left Books, 1981) p. 92.

9 William H. Branson and Helen B. Junz, "Trends in U.S. Trade and Compar-

ative Advantage," *Brookings Papers on Economic Activity No. 2*, (Washington, D.C.: The Brookings Institution, 1971) p. 285.

10 *New York Times*, March 1, 1984, D1; *New York Times*, April 8, 1986, D8f.

11 See, James Fallows, "The Spend-Up," *The Atlantic*, Vol. 258 No. 1.

12 See, for example, *Business Week*, September 3, 1990, pp. 48–50.

13 Thomas C. Schelling, *Strategy of Conflict* (New York: Oxford University Press, 1960) pp. 11–12.

14 Stephen D. Krasner, "Structural causes and regime consequences: Regimes as intervening variables," *International Organization* Vol. 36, No. 2, Spring 1982, p. 186.

15 For further details on the geographical distribution of Japan's Official Development Assistance, see, *Japans Official Development Assistance 1988 Annual Report* (Tokyo: Ministry of Foreign Affairs, 1988) pp. 43–47.

16 Elaine Kurtenbach, "Trade frictions worse than ever," *Tampa Tribune*, Sunday, December 3, 1989, p. 1-E.

17 Akio Morita and Shintaro Ishihata, *The Japan That Can Say No* (Tokyo: Kobunsha Publishing Co., 1989).

18 David E. Sanger, *New York Times*; *Tampa Tribune*, "U.S. offers Japan a partnership on supercollider," Friday, June 1, 1990, p. 13-A.

19 A *Los Angeles Times* Report; *Tampa Tribune*, "U.S., Japan strike deal on trade reforms," Friday, June 29, 1990, p 2-A.

20 *Tampa Tribune*, "Japan builds up defense despite European thaw," Sunday, December 10, 1989, p. 25-A.

21 Robert O. Keohane, *After Hegemony: Cooperation and Discord in the - World Political Economy* (Princeton, NJ: Princeton University Press, 1984) pp. 136-7.

22 Robert O. Keohane, *After Hegemony: Cooperation and Discord in the - World Political Economy*, p. 141, p. 178.

23 *International Legal Materials* 1975, "Agreement on an International Energy Program," 12 (1): 1–35.

24 *International Legal Materials* 1974, "Communique on the Washington Energy Conference," 13(2): p. 462.

25 See, for example, Henry A. Kissinger, *Years of Upheaval* (Boston: Little, Brown, 1982).

26 U.S. Department of State, 1973, "The United States and a Unifying Europe: The Necessity of Partnership," *Department of State Bulletin* 69 (1801), p. 781.

27 Weekly Compilation of Presidential Documents, 1974, "Washington Energy Conference," 10(7), pp. 201–202.

28 Peter Truell, "Price Comparison May Cost Japanese In Trade Discussions," *Wall Street Journal*, 8 November 1989: A8.

CONCLUSION: TOWARD A SYSTEM OF COLLECTIVE
HEGEMONIC RESPONSIBILITY

The objective of this book is to analyze the changing international roles of the United States and Japan, and identify the emerging trends in their relationship as it is shaped and conditioned by Japan's phenomenal power economic capabilities on the one hand, and the United States eroding hegemony on the other. In chapter one we presented the theoretical framework for this study and argued that Japan's increasing push for globalism manifested in its aid, trade and investment activities, its entanglements in Third World regional conflicts, its overall efforts to satisfy international expectations, are a function of its enormous power economic capabilities, and the transition from United States hegemonic leadership to a relationship of mutual power-dependence with Japan. We attempted to apply this framework and its components to Japan's globalist behavior and the U.S.-Japan relations in: (1) the area of economic activities in developing countries; (2) technological interdependence; (3) the evolving new security relationship; and (4) the major arguments of hegemonic stability theory.

In the preceding chapters it has been repeatedly suggested that positive cooperative U.S.-Japan relations must be understood in terms of United States' overwhelming economic dominance up until the early 1970s, and in terms of its post-World War II strategy of containing the Soviet threat. A stable liberal international economic order and a stable U.S.-Japan relationship was perceived by policymakers as vital to the strength of the Western alliance. The current "turbulent" character of the international system could undermine the liberal international economic order in general, and U.S.-Japan bilateral relations in particular. In the past two decades Japan's economic power has been steadily internationalized to the extent that the U.S.-Japan relationship has been underpinned by a new interdependence characterized by a substantial decline in the hegemonic functions of the United States, and a corresponding growth in the power economic capabilities of Japan.

Japan's resource diplomacy manifested in foreign aid, for example, promotes interdependence with developing countries and its underlying factors of access to raw materials, markets, and investment outlets.   One of the imperatives of economic globalism is that, at times, Japan is caught between a two-way power-dependence: on the one hand, is its close ties with the United States, and on the other hand, is its need to strengthen political ties with oil-rich nations even in the face of policy divergence with the United States. Economic expansionism tends to intersect conflictually with political realities in volatile and explosive regions of the world thereby creating dilemmas for Japan.   At times, bilateral U.S.-Japan relationships tend to manifest themselves in constructive collaboration efforts of mutual benefit as in Japan's complementary role in Panama, Nicaragua, or the Philippines. Japan's foreign aid to developing countries, for example, may be performing a dual function: an instrument for commercial penetration and a vehicle to realize U.S. foreign policy objectives.   Furthermore, the complementary character of Japan's foreign aid in relation to the shrinking U.S. economic aid package helps to maintain the liberal international economic status quo. The complementary role of Japanese foreign aid to U.S. regional objectives is an element of mutual power-dependence between the two nations because: (1) Japan and the U.S. often have compatible regional interests; and (2) the compatibility or congruence of interests is structured by common perceived threats to their national security.

In this era of deconcentration of hegemony, Japan's power economic capabilities are undergoing rapid geographic diversification to include more of Africa and Latin America.   The push for diversification is being motivated especially by the trend toward regional blocs and the fear of protectionism. The turbulence in the global system is partly manifested in certain conflictual aspects of U.S.-Japan relations such as in the area of technology where three interactive dimensions could be identified: a structural dimension (ongoing changes in the relative technological capabilities of the two nations), a procedural dimension (ongoing changes in the institutions and procedures around which the two nations expectations on technological issues converge, and a "substantive" dimension (changes in the actual bilateral expectations of the two nations on science and technology issues). The analysis in this book suggests that there is turbulence in the Japanese-American relationship manifested in the various issue-areas: trade, technology, military security, foreign aid, and so on.

A new security relationship is steadily evolving characterized not by the patron-client (U.S.-Japan) relationship of the early 1980s but by a relationship of mutual security-dependence based on a partnership whose function is to maintain peace and stability in developing regions, in particular. Japan's obvious military security importance is based on its growing dynamism in the area of advanced high technology components relevant to U.S. weapons systems. Mutual security-dependence involves getting Japan to assume its fair share of burdens that are commensurate with its power economic capabilities. The convergence of three trends—the end of the Cold War, Japan's rapid ascent as an economic superpower, and the perceived relative economic decline of the United States—have brought into sharper focus the debate about Japan's current and future international role. The major premise of hegemonic stability theory, that of a significant decline in U.S. hegemony, points to an evolving "adversarial cooperation" relationship because of the U.S. pressure to adjust its policies to slow down the process of decline and account for the cost of defending the hegemonic order. The premise of a significant decline in U.S. hegemony implies a corresponding decrease in the remunerative economic capabilities of the United States, prompting positive cooperation in the form of Japan, and others, supplying significant economic capabilities to effect hegemonic outcomes around the world, such as in the recent Persian Gulf War.

With the turbulent international system and the profound changes in the U.S.-Japan bilateral relationship in mind, we can now provide an alternative conceptualization of the emerging global order in general and the U.S.-Japan relationship in particular, one that takes into account political, military, economic, and technological concerns and interdependence between the United States, Japan, and other advanced industrial countries.

First, we will argue that a new structure of world power distribution is unfolding. Second, we will elaborate from our empirical observations on the structure and rules for new roles. Significant global developments caused the new structure of power to develop; the relative equality between the United States, Japan, and other advanced industrial nations did not develop because of the new structure. Far-reaching systemic changes are placing the most industrially advanced countries in the same situation, that of mutual, inescapable systemic vulnerability. They have two choices: they could opt to ignore this "trend" acting as if the structure is still one in which the U.S. is still the hegemonic leader; or they could recognize the full implications of the risks involved in the evolving structure and construct rules to collectively manage or respond to the new situation in recognition of their mutual and common interests.

Collective Hegemonic Responsibility

Many perspectives—system supporter, leader supporter, system-wide cooperation, and so on—have already been put forward regarding the changed or evolving leadership role of the United States and the current economic super-power status of Japan in the international system.[1] However, in the performance of hegemonic functions like world's financial stabilizer, foremost aid donor, strongest military power, and technological leader, it is reasonable to view such hegemonic functions in terms of the notion of collective systemic responsibility among the most advanced industrial nations, or some sort of collective management of hegemony. Four factors underlie a system of collective responsibility for the global economic order. First, no nation in the international system is in a dominant position and fulfills the criteria of military power, political strength, economic strength, and cultural universality, criteria necessary for hegemonic power status. Second, the deconcentration of hegemonic capabilities—military power, economic power, technological power, and so on—among the major industrial nations puts one or the other in advantageous positions (a kind of power disequilibrium) to assume leadership in specific power domains until conditions change. Third, the interdependence underlying a specific power domain compels the domain leaders to exercise leadership based on mutual interest to maintain system stability. Fourth, the instability inherent in the global economic order and the dynamism involved in the collective leadership structure require that the collective leadership co-ordinate, exchange, and reevaluate leadership positions (financial leader, foremost aid donor, technological leader, or foremost military power) from time to time and when necessary.

Next, we attempt to relate four basic global systemic functions—financial stabilizer, foreign aid-giving, military security guarantor, and technological leadership—to the notion of collective hegemonic responsibility in the global order, and to the U.S.-Japan relationship in particular. The most important conclusion of this analysis is that the current trend in the global economic order and in U.S.-Japan interactions could best be conceptualized as basically evolving towards a system of collectively managed hegemony structured by collective hegemonic responsibility. The new structure of collective hegemonic leadership responsibility will be based on four major principles: (1) a *primus inter pares* in each of four functional prerequisites (financial stability, foreign aid flows, military security, technological leadership) of a sound global economic order; (2) an emphasis on co-equality and the rejection of rivalry for dominance in political, economic, military, or technological issues; (3) a recognition of mutual vulnerability, since excessive economic nationalism could lead to systems collapse, reminiscent of the 1930s; and (4) a willingness, and the existence of a forum (institutions), to revise, and renegotiate rules until an acceptable minimum is reached. This framework is dynamic and not static because leadership is assumed to change hands based on the dynamism of the individual national economies of the collective leadership in the specific functional prerequisites outlined above.

The core of the new structure is the avoidance of mutual vulnerability caused by excessive economic nationalism reminiscent of the 1920s and 1930s. This could mean an increase in the number of rules and agreements relevant to the efficient functioning of the four functional prerequisites of a stable international economic system. In international political economy parlance, each of the new arrangements or rules can be conceptualized as distinct regimes centering on the political, economic, and military security of the global economic order. The end result is a collective, comprehensive, multilateral, global security regime, originating from the most powerful nations of the international system. Moreover, because no single hegemonic leader is available, the mutual interest of the major powers to maintain an open and stable international economic order will motivate them to create and maintain a collectively "managed" hegemonic system through burden sharing on the four essential variables of: (1) financial stability; (2) foreign aid disbursements; (3) military security; and (4) technological innovation. The collective leadership, because of the enormous power economic and politico-military capabilities of its members will be prepared to negotiate, make concessions, or in game-theoretic language, cooperate or defect in the interest of a stable world order and in their own collective self-interest. That is, a sense of collective hegemonic responsibility arises out of mutual and common interests; multilateral institutions uniting the various leaders will play a role in mitigating the natural proclivities toward excessive self-interested behavior detrimental to other members of the collective, promoting a greater degree of compliance with rules that serve the interests of its members as well as of the global system.

Although realist scholars emphasize the anarchic nature of the international system, what is striking about the behavior of states in this anarchy is the extent to which they comply with bilateral and multilateral agreements binding them, not the few instances in which they disregard them outrightly. Even when states disregard or dispute over rules, they usually leave room for revision, replacement, or renegotiation of new rules.

A structure of collectively managed hegemony obviously translates into a closely "guided interdependence" with its own set of problems.[2] From the international relations standpoint, the problem is how to benefit from international transactions while maintaining as much interdependence as possible. Normally states operate on the basis of shifting a disproportionate share of the burdens of interdependence on to others while retaining as much freedom of action, and a disproportionate share of rewards as possible. From the perspective of the global system, the problem is how to generate and maintain a mutually beneficial process of collective hegemonic responsibility, in the face of competing efforts by state and non-state actors to maintain the system for their own benefit.

The single most important conflict between state interests and the needs of the global economic order is over state autonomy. For example, as the 1991 Persian Gulf crisis vividly illustrated, states' interests in military competition with other states clash directly with the interests of global capitalism in the normal conduct of national and international commerce. Yet, analysts have also noted that because of their economic interests, nineteenth century European states behaved with unprecedented restraint. Karl Polanyi, for example, attributed the "one hundred years' peace" in Europe mostly to the activities of international capitalism and only partly to the interests of major states in suppressing revolution.[3]

The behavior of states in relation to international regimes is a special manifestation of a clash of interests between the state and system requirements. In the case of collective hegemonic responsibility, regimes may be overwhelmingly representative of the perceived interests of the collective leadership as well as the interests of the subordinate states in the system. As long as the collective leadership maintains system stability through mutual self-interest it can revise, recreate, or modify regimes to suit the vicissitudes of the global economic order. Thus, a system of collective hegemonic responsibility (collectively "managed hegemony") becomes the creation of the dominant states in the international system and, as such, constitutes an arena for "guided competition" among its members and those outside.

Elements of Co-Equal Responsibility

The first principle is the principle of co-equal status of the collective hegemonic leadership, except in a functional area (aid, technology, finance, or military security) where one becomes the *primus inter pares*. It would mean a willingness by Japan and future economic superpowers to assume responsibility commensurate with their economic power. On the other hand, it would also mean a willingness on the part of the United States to concede leadership in many functional areas in the interest of mutual security. Second, is the willingness by members of the collective leadership to relinquish some elements of power to others when conditions realistically change, and the willingness by a new nation to assume responsibility and effectively play the role of *primus inter pares* in a specific functional area. In the absence of this willingness, the first rule is invalidated. The United States could, for example, relinquish leadership in the International Monetary Fund or World Bank to Japan, if Japan's foremost financial status becomes both a necessary and sufficient condition for a change in leadership.

Third, out of security self-interest the collective leadership should abjure from economic practices (especially in trade and technology) that could undermine the economic foundation of another member's economy. In other words, the stability of another nation's society is in the interest of other members as well. Japan, for example, will show some constraint in its trade interactions with other members and vice versa. Finally, an institutionalized negotiation and renegotiation process should be maintained to uphold the new structure. Maintenance of the new collective structure means ongoing trade and finance negotiations to settle differences and work out more effective arrangements. They will range from bilateral, multilateral, to summit meetings.

Collective management of hegemony implies the pursuit of a balanced internationalism, as opposed to a lopsided globalism that emphasizes only the outflow of capital, exports and companies to other countries. A balanced globalism is based on an open economy with equal emphasis on the outflow and inflow of finance, capital, people and companies to other nations. The size and economic might of the financial *primus inter pares* gives it the capacity to provide and maintain the confidence necessary for a stable international monetary system and its currency serves as a source of liquidity for an increasingly open system. Or the focus could be on creating confidence in a monetary system where adequate liquidity would be provided by a collectively agreed upon national currencies. As a system of collective hegemony, their productivity creates price advantages in their favor, and it should be in their interest to impose "free trade" on the world economy because they are the most cost-efficient producers. Because they dominate the world economy, their collective interests are focused on maintaining the global status quo and to opposing any intra-core wars that might upset their dominant position. They even also oppose any intra-periphery crises (for example Iraq's invasion of Kuwait) that has the potential of upsetting their dominant position.

In the more recent rhetoric between the United States and Japan, there are strong indications that the two nations are inching more towards an attitude of collective responsibility for system stability, that may even be bordering on a willingness, on the part of the United States, for power sharing with Japan. For example, in March 1990, President Bush said:

> There are three things that are very clear to me: that our relationship with Japan will become even more important to us and to the world in the coming decades; that Japan is moving rapidly to assume a leading role in the world, as was evident in Prime Minister Kaifu's recent trip to Eastern Europe, and the nearly $2 billion in assistance that he pledged to the nations of Poland and Hungary; and that no matter where we look around the world—from Eastern Europe to Panama to Cambodia—the United States and Japan are working together to promote political and economic transformations that will strengthen democracies and market economies.

The Japanese Prime Minister, Kaifu, in turn responded positively to Bush's characterization of the U.S.-Japan relationship as of paramount global importance. Kaifu said:

> U.S.-Japanese relations today, transcending our bilateral framework, have acquired the significance of a global partnership with responsibilities for tasks facing the world. The President and I welcomed that the Japan-U.S. global partnership is bearing specific fruit in such a broad range of fields as the response to regional problems, the management of world economy, economic cooperation for developing countries and debt problems, environment, drugs and the fight against international terrorism.[4]

Statements by both leaders reflect an attitude of collective hegemonic responsibility for global order. Gradually and reluctantly, we see signs of the U.S. giving up its insistence on dominance. As this process continues to advance, the opportunity will arise for the United States, Japan and other advanced industrial nations to transform the new structure of global power into a multilateral security arrangement based on a principle of collective hegemonic responsibility structured by the functional prerequisites for a stable international economic order.

The threat of economic dislocation may, in the short run, constrain a dependent partner (Japan or the United States) from executing foreign policies that are against its partner's strategic interests. However, if one partner is determined to execute policies that are detrimental to the other partner's interests, it must develop alternative economic partners over the long-term. Its challenge, then, is to find an equally viable economic partner.

A game-theoretical model of the uncertainty in the global economic order and in U.S.-Japan relations is provided by the Prisoners' Dilemma, in which the "defection" of two prisoners (that is the admittance of guilt) results in criminal sentences that "cooperation" could have avoided. Prisoners' Dilemma suggests that, so long as Japan refuses to engage in burden sharing with the United States commensurate with its power, the United States will also refuse to maintain its traditional role in the relationship, despite the overall detrimental effects. Our argument is based on the suggestion that U.S.-Japan bilateral management of hegemony, or collective responsibility for a stable global economic order depends upon: the ability of the collective leadership to serve as a system stabilizer of last resort; and the common interest perceptions regarding the nature and extent of the threat to their collective security. In the 1991 Persian Gulf War, both conditions were operative and thus the U.S. and Japan, and other advanced industrial nations, exhibited a high degree of collective system management. Conversely, in 1973-74 during the Yom Kippur War and subsequent Arab oil embargo, common interest perceptions between the two nations differed. However, in terms of co-equal status, collective responsibility, or collective hegemonic leadership, it is likely that as the U.S. continues to face difficulty in finding financial resources to share with its allies in developing countries, Japan's and other allies' resource commitment will increase the pressure for political commitment. In fact, as Japan's ODA becomes an increasingly important element of its share of the security burden, the aid begins to represent Japan's political commitment to the United States for the maintenance of a stable international system.

Finally, this analysis would be incomplete without adequately underscoring the status and role of Multinational Corporations in the contemporary global political economy and in a system of collectively managed hegemony. In our contemporary international system in particular, nation states are not the only actors in the international political economy; they are not the only nodes in the network of major actors that must be taken into account in delineating the key elements of a collectively managed hegemonic system. Significant actions and transactions made by MNCs, for example, are not all subsumed within the trade statistics of one or another nation state. In fact, many MNCs are engaged in transactions of greater dollar value than the entire trade of many nation states.[5] Moreover, they make major decisions about the disposition of the goods and services under their control, decisions that affect even the objectives of the advanced industrial countries where most of them originate. In other words, our international system is characterized by both international and supranational activities—states do certain things, corporations and other entities do other things, and there are interrelationships among the two kinds of units. This unity of process and structure is what Alvin Wolfe refers to as "a system at a supranational level of integration"[6]—a complex of ties linking firms, governments, various institutions, and even persons. Joint ventures are a good example of such supranational integration, and states are often partners in these joint ventures.

The power and influence of MNCs are so pervasive in the international system that complex interdependence theorists argue that the MNC is, by far, one of those entities that is making the nation state an anachronism. The state's control over economic affairs will continually give way to the MNC and other international institutions.[7] The MNC is integrating national economies in the areas of trade, money, production, investment and marketing. The transnational intermeshing of interests and the recognized benefits and detrimental effects of economic interdependence are enhanced by the pervasiveness of MNCs. In a positive sense, the MNC is becoming more capable and effective than the nation state in providing employment, regional development, and other benefits that accompany direct foreign investment.

Multinational Corporations, in another sense, could be viewed as a key element of the global structure of power and influence that control assets in virtually all countries. Their worldwide direct investment stocks (that is, amount already in place) rose from $67 billion in 1960 to $714 billion in 1985. In the 1980s, the six hundred largest industrial MNCs accounted for between one-fifth and one-fourth of the global production of goods. They, in large part, control global trade, in some cases controlling 80 per cent to 90 per cent of exports from advanced industrial countries.[8] Many MNCs are among the world's largest economic units, and are characterized by oligopolistic aspirations.

Nation states and MNCs complement each other sufficiently in terms of economic and political capabilities. The former is endowed with territory and a source of raw materials, whereas the latter has under its control capital, technology, and access to world markets. Converging or common interests and functions between the two entities, among others, include: (1) the aggregation of investment capital that can fund development; (2) underwriting R&D that leads to technological innovation; (3) specifically promoting growth and modernization in developing countries; (4) promoting free trade and lobbying for the removal of barriers to trade; (5) speeding up the internationalization of the global economy and culture through promotion of rules governing international commerce; and (6) increasing the volume of international trade. In politics or foreign policy, MNCs have indirectly served as instruments through which the state has pursued its foreign policy objectives. In the realm of economic sanctions, for example, foreign subsidiaries of American based MNCs have at times been used by the U.S. government to implement trade embargoes against other nations. Similarly MNCs have also been used to enhance U.S. intelligence gathering capabilities in foreign lands. In such instances, state interests and the interests of MNCs have tended to converge benefitting both entities in the process. Both entities contribute largely to blurring the boundaries between internal and external politico-economic affairs.

The enormous power economic capabilities of the MNCs, their pervasiveness in the global economy, and their many common interests with the states that make up the collective hegemonic leadership, are elements that are central to a collectively managed hegemonic system. Each *primus inter pares* could effect its leadership in its respective domain by encouraging collaborative efforts with the giant MNCs of the global system. The common and converging functions and interests are nurtured and developed towards a supranational integration and collective management of hegemony in the realms of financial stability, foreign aid flows, military security, and technological innovation. The current wave of politics and economics in the Third World and former Communist bloc points to the creation of a more democratic and capitalist-oriented environment. An environment that, no doubt, will become progressively conducive to the political, economic, and military objectives of a collective leadership by major capitalist countries and giant Multinational Corporations.

Endnotes

1 For further details on roles related to hegemony and the evolving global order, see Syed Javed Maswood, *Japan and protection: The growth of protectionist sentiment and the Japanese response* (London: Routledge, 1989); and Takashi Inoguchi, "Japan's Global Role in a Multipolar World," in Shafiqul Islam (ed.) *Yen For Development* (New York: Council on Foreign Relations Press, 1991).

2 For a discussion of the various conceptualizations of interdependence, see, Robert O. Keohane and Joseph S. Nye, Jr., *Power and Interdependence: World Politics in Transition* (Boston: Little, Brown, 1977); David A. Baldwin, "Interdependence and Power: A Conceptual Analysis," *International Organization* Vol. 34, No. 4 (1980), pp 471–506; and K.J. Holsti, *The Dividing Discipline: Hegemony and Diversity in International Theory* (Winchester, Mass: Allen and Unwin, 1985).

3 Karl Polanyi, *The Great Transformation: The Political and Economic Origins of Our Time* (New York: Farrar and Reinhart, 1944).

4 Statements by U.S. President, George Bush, and the then newly-elected Japanese Prime Minister, Toshiki Kaifu, at the conclusion of their hurriedly scheduled "desert summit" in Palm Springs, on March 2-3, 1990.

5 For details on the economic dominance of MNCs, see, among other works Barry B. Hughes, *Continuity and Change in World Politics: The Clash of Perspectives* (Englewood Cliffs: Prentice Hall, 1991) pp. 362–372; Raymond Vernon, *Sovereignty at Bay* (New York: Basic Books, 1971); and Richard J. Bennet, and Ronald E. Muller, *Global Reach: The Power of the Multinational Corporation* (New York: Simon and Schuster, 1974).

6 Alvin Wolfe, "Effects of Multinational Enterprises on Supranational Networks," paper presented at the SunBelt Social Network Conference, Clearwater Beach, Florida, February 13, 1987, p. 7.

7 Details on arguments along the lines of the future roles of multinational corporations vis-a-vis the nation-state are found in Robert Gilpin, "Three Models of the Future," *International Organization* 29 (Winter 1975), pp. 37–60.

8 United Nations Centre on Transnational Corporations, *Transnational Corporations in World Development: Trends and Prospects* (New York: United Nations Centre on Transnational Corporations, 1988), pp. 14–25; 76–77.

BIBLIOGRAPHY

Books

Agbi, Sunday O. *Japan's Attitudes and Policies Towards African Issues Since 1945: A Historical Perspective* (Tokyo: Institute of Developing Economies, 1982) V.R.F. Series No. 96.

Allen, G.C. *A Short Economic History of Modern Japan* (New York: Praeger Publishers, 1962).

Axelford, Robert. *The Evolution of Cooperation* (New York: Basic Books, 1984).

Balassa, Bela and Marcus Noland. *Japan in the World Economy* (Institute for International Economics, 1988).

Baldwin, David A. *Economic Statecraft* (Princeton: Princeton University Press, 1985).

Baldwin, Robert. "The New Protectionism: A Response to Shifts in National Economic Power," in Jeffrey A. Frieden and David A. Lake (eds.). *International Political Economy Perspectives on Global Power and Wealth* (New York: St. Martins, 1991).

Barnet, Richard J. and Ronald E. Muler. Global Reach: The Power of the Multisectional Corporation (New York: Simon and Schuster, 1974).

Barnett, Robert W.. *Beyond War: Japan's Concept of Comprehensive National Security* (Washington, D.C.: Pergamon-Brassey's, 1984).

Becker, W.H. and S.F. Wells Jr. (eds.) *Economics and World Power: An Assessment of American Diplomacy Since 1789* (New York: Columbia University Press, 1984).

Block, Julia Chang. "A United States-Japan Aid Alliance?," in Shafiqul Islam (ed.) *Yen for Development: Japanese Foreign Aid and the Politics of Burden Sharing* (New York: Council on Foreign Relations Press, 1991).

Bloom, Justin L. "The United States-Japan Bilateral Science and Technology Relationship: A Personal Evaluation," in Mitchell B. Wallerstein, (ed.) *Scientific and Technological Cooperation Among Industrialized Countries: The Role of the United States* (Washington, D.C.: National Academy Press, 1984).

_____. "A New Era for United States-Japanese Technical Relations?" in Cecil H. Uyehara (ed.) *United States-Japanese Science and Technology Exchange Patterns of Interdependence* (Boulder: Westview Press, 1988).

Burks, Ardath W. *Japan: A Postindustrial Power* (Boulder: Westview Press, 1984).

Busch, Noel F. *The Horizon Concise History of Japan* (New York: American Heritage Publishing Co., 1972).

Chander, Alfred Dupont. *The Visible Hand: The Managerial Revolution in American Business* (Cambridge: Harvard University Press, 1982).

Close, Upton. *Behind the Face of Japan* (New York: Appleton-Century Co., 1942.)

Conteh-Morgan, Earl. *American Foreign Aid and Global Power Projection—The Geopolitics of Resource Allocation* (Aldershot: Dartmouth Publishing Company, 1990).

Cooper, Richard N. *The Economics of Interdependence* (New York: McGraw-Hill for the Council on Foreign Relations, 1968).

Cowhey, Peter F. "The Agenda of the Leading Nations for the World Economy: A Theory of International Economic Regimes," in Gunther Heiduk and Kozo Yamamura (eds.). *Technological Competition and Interdependence: The Search for Policy in the United States, West Germany, and Japan* (Seattle: University of Washington Press, 1990).

Cox, Robert W. "Production and Hegemony: Toward a Political Economy of World Order," in Harold K. Jacobsen and Dusan Sidjanski (eds.) *The Emerging Industrial Economic Order* (Beverley Hills: Sage Publications, 1982).

Dineen, Gerald P. "United States-Japan: A Comparative Assessment," in Cecil H. Uyehara (ed.) *United States-Japan Science and Technology Exchange Patterns of Interdependence* (Boulder: Westview Press, 1988).

Drifte, Reinhard. *Japan's Foreign Policy* (London: The Royal Institute of International Affairs, 1990).

Eto, Hajime. "Behavior of Japanese R & D Organizations," in Hajime Eto and Konomu Matsui (eds.) *R&D Management Systems in Japanese Industry* (Amsterdam: North Holland Company, 1984).

Frost, Ellen. *For Richer, For Poorer: The New United States-Japan Relationship* (New York: Council on Foreign Relations, 1987).

Funabashi, Yoichi. *Keizai anzenhosho: Chikyukeizai jidai no pawa ekonomikkusu* (Power economics in the age of global economy) (Tokyo: Tokyokeizai Shimposha, 1978).

Galbraith, John K. *The Anatomy of Power* (Boston: Houghton Mifflin Co. 1983).

Gilpin, Robert. *United States Power and Multinational Corporations* (New York: Basic Books, 1975).

_____. *War and Change in World Politics* (Cambridge: Cambridge University Press, 1981).

_____. *The Political Economy of International Relations* (Princeton: Princeton University Press, 1987).

Gowa, J. *Closing the Gold Window: Domestic Politics and the End of Bretton Woods* (Ithaca, New York: Cornell University Press, 1983).

Harris, Martha. "Japan's International Technology Transfers," *Japan's economy and trade with the United States* (Washington, D.C.: Joint Economic Committee, Congress of the United States, Dec. 9, 1985).

Holsti, K.J. *The Dividing Discipline: Hegemony and Diversity in International Theory* (Winchester, Mass.: Allen and Urwin, 1985).

Hughes, Barry B. *Continuity and Change in World Politics: The Clash of Perspectives* (Englewood Cliffs: Prentice Hall, 1991).

Inoguchi, Takashi. "Four Japanese Scenarios for the Future," in Jeffrey A. Frieden and David A. Lake (eds.) *International Political Economy Perspectives on Global Power and Wealth* (New York: St. Martins Press, 1991).

_____. "Japan's Global Role in a Multipolar World," in Shafigul Islam (ed.) *Yen for Development: Japanese Foreign Aid and the Politics of Burden Sharing* (New York: Council on Foreign Relations Press, 1991).

Iriye, Akira and Warren Cohen (eds.). *The United States and Japan in the Postwar World* (Lexington: The University of Kentucky Press, 1988).

Ishikawa, Kenjiro. *Japan and the Challenge of Europe 1992* (London: Pinter Publishers, 1990).

Kennedy, Paul. *The Rise and Fall of the Great Powers* (London: Unwin and Hyman, 1988).

Keohane, Robert O. *After Hegemony: Cooperation and Discord in the World Political Economy* (Princeton: Princeton University Press, 1984).

Keohane, Robert O. and Joseph S. Nye, Jr. *Power and Interdependence: World Politics in Transition* (Boston: Little, Brown, 1977).

Kindelberger, Charles P. *The World in Depression 1929–1939* (Berkeley: University of California Press, 1986).

_____. *Power and Money: The Economics of International Politics and the Politics of International Economics* (New York: Basic Books, 1970).

Kishimoto, Koichi. *Politics in Modern Japan: Development and Organization* (Tokyo: Japan Echo, 1978).

Kissinger, Henry A. *Years of Upheaval* (Boston, Mass.: Little, Brown, 1982).

Kosaka, Masataka. *Japan's Choices: New Globalism and Cultural Orientations in an Industrial State* (London: Pinter Publishers, 1989).

Krasner, Stephen D. "Structural causes and regime consequences: Regimes as intervening variables," in Stephen D. Krasner (ed.), *International Regimes* (Ithaca: Cornell University Press, 1983).

Kurian, George Thomas. *Facts on File: National Profiles Japan* (New York: Facts on File, Inc., 1990).

Lake, David A. "International Economic Structure and American Economic Foreign Policy, 1887–1934," in Jeffrey A. Frieden and David A. Lake, (eds.) *International Political Economy* (New York: St. Martins Press, 1991).

Latourette, Kenneth. *The History of Japan* (New York: The MacMillan Co., 1957).

Lincoln, Edward. *Japan's Unequal Trade* (Brookings Institution, 1990).

Mason, R.H.P. and J.G. Caiger. *A History of Japan* (New York: The Free Press, 1972).

Maswood, Syed Javed. *Japan and Protection The growth of protectionist sentiment and the Japanese response* (London: Routledge, 1989).

McCulloch, Rachel. "The Challenge to United States Leadership in High Technology Industries: Can the United States Maintain Its Lead? Should It Try?" in Gunther Heiduk and Kozo Yamamura (eds.) *Technological Competition and Interdependence* (Seattle: University of Washington Press, 1990).

Meyer, Milton W. *Japan A Concise History* (Boston: Allyn and Bacon, Inc., 1966).

Morita, Akio and Shintaro Ishibata. *The Japan That Can Say No* (Tokyo: Kobunsha Publishing Co., 1989).

Morse, Ronald A. (ed.). *Japan and the Middle East in Alliance Politics* (The Wilson Center: International Security Studies Program, 1986).

Morse, Ronald A. and S. Yoshida (eds.) *Blind Partners: American and Japanese Responses to an Unknown Future* (Maryland: University Press of America, 1985).

Nelson, Joan M. *Aid, Influence and Foreign Policy* (New York: Macmillan, 1968).

Nelson, Richard R. "What Has Happened to United States Technological Leadership," in Gunther Heiduk and Kozo Yamamura (eds.) *Technological Competition and Interdependence The Search for Policy in the United States, West Germany, and Japan* (Seattle: University of Washington Press, 1990).

Nelson, Richard N. (ed.) *Government and Technical Progress: A Cross-Industry Analysis* (New York: Pergamon Press, 1982).

Noland, Marcus. *Japan in the World Economy* (Washington: Institute for International Economics, 1988).

Nye, Joseph S. Jr. *Bound to Lead: The Changing Nature of American Power* (New York: Basic Books, Inc., 1990).

Oda, Hideo and Kazuyoski Aoki. "Japan and Africa: Beyond the Fragile Partnership," in Robert S. Ozaki and Walter Arnold (eds.) *Japan's Foreign*

Relation: A Global Search for Economic Security (Boulder: Westview Press, 1985).

Okawara, Yoshio. *To Avoid Isolation: An Ambassador's Views of United States-Japanese Relations* (Columbia: University of South Carolina Press, 1990).

Okimoto, Daniel and Gary Saxonhouse. "Technology and the Future of the Economy," in Kozo Yamamura and Yasukichi Yasuba (eds.) *The Political Economy of Japan: Domestic Transformation* (Stanford, Calif.: Stanford University Press, 1987).

Olsen, Edward A. *United States-Japan strategic reciprocity: a neo-nationalist view* (Stanford, Calif.: Hoover Institution Press, 1985).

Ozaki, Robert S. and Walter Arnold. *Japan's Foreign Relations A Global Search for Economic Security* (Boulder: Westview Press, 1985).

Pempel, T.J. (ed.) *Policymaking in Contemporary Japan* (Ithaca, New York: Cornell University Press, 1977).

Parboni, Ricardo. *The Dollar and Its Rivals* (London: New Left Books, 1981).

_____. *Policy and Politics in Japan: Creative Conservatism* (Philadelphia: Temple University Press, 1982).

Polanyi, Karl. *The Great Transformation: The Political and Economic Origins of Our Time* (New York: Farvar and Reinhart, 1974).

Policinksi, Mark R. "The Japanese Technical Literature Act of 1986," in Cecil H. Uyehara (ed.) *United States-Japan Science and Technology Exchange Patterns of Interdependence* (Boulder: Westview Press, 1988).

Rapkin, David. *World Leadership and Hegemony* (Boulder, Co.: Lynne Rienner, 1990).

Reischauer, Edwin O. *The Japanese* (Cambridge, Mass.: Belnap-Harvard University Press, 1978).

_____. *The Japanese Today* (Cambridge: Harvard University Press, 1989).

_____. *Japan: The Story of a Nation* (New York: Alfred Knopf, 1974).

Roberts, Brad. *The New Democracies: Global Change and United States Policy* (Cambridge: MIT Press, 1991).

Rosecrance, Richard. *America's Economic Resurgence: A Bold New Strategy* (New York: Harper and Row, 1990).

_____. *America as an Ordinary Country* (Ithaca: Cornell University Press, 1976).

Rosenau, James N. *Turbulence in World Politics A Theory of Change and Continuity* (Princeton: Princeton University Press, 1991).

Rowland, B.M. (ed.) *Balance of Power or Hegemony: The Inter-War Monetary System* (New York: Alfred A. Knopf, 1976).

Saxonhouse, Gary. "Technological Progress and R&D Systems in Japan and the United States," in Cecil H. Uyehara (ed.) *United States-Japan Science and Technology Exchange Patterns of Interdependence* (Boulder: Westview Press, 1988).

_____. "Industrial Policy and Factor Markets," in Hugh Patrick (ed.), *Japan's High Technology Industries* (Seattle: University of Washington Press, 1986).

Scalapino, Robert A. (ed.) *The Foreign Policy of Modern Japan* (Berkeley and Los Angeles: University of California Press, 1977).

Schelling, Thomas C. *Strategy of Conflict* (New York: Oxford University Press, 1960).

Shively, Donald H. *Tradition and Modernization in Japanese Culture* (Princeton: Princeton University Press, 1971).

Sterner, Michael. "The Middle East Factor in United States-Japanese Relations," in Ronald A. Morse (ed.) *Japan and the Middle East in Alliance Politics* (The Wilson Center: International Security Studies Program, 1986).

Strange, Susan. "Still an extraordinary power: America's role in the global monetary system," in R. Lomba and R. Witte, (eds.) *The Political Economy of International and Domestic Monetary Relations* (Ames: Iowa State University Press, 1982).

Takeyasu, Yoshimitsu. "Science and Technology Policy in Japan," in Cecil H. Uyehara (ed.) *United States-Japan Science and Technology Exchange Patterns of Interdependence* (Boulder: Westview Press, 1988).

Turin, G. et al. *JTECH Panel Report on Telecommunications: Technology in Japan* (LaJolla, Calif.: Science Applications International Corporation, May 1986).

Vernon, Raymond. *Sovereignty at Bay* (New York: Basic Books, 1971).

Waltz, Kenneth N.   "The Myth of National Interdependence," in Charles Kindelberger, (ed.) *The International Corporation* (Cambridge, Mass.: MIT Press, 1970).

Yoshitsu, Michael M.   "The Strategic Costs of Oil Dependence," in Ronald A. Morse (ed.) *Japan and the Middle East in Alliance Politics* (The Wilson Center: International Security Studies, 1986).

_____. *Caught in the Middle East* (Toronto: Lexington Books, 1984).

Young, O.R. (ed.)   *Bargaining: Formal Theories of Negotiation* (Chicago: University of Illinois Press, 1975).

Journals

Akaha, Tsuneo.   "Japanese Security Policy after United States Hegemony," *Millennium*, Vol. 18, No. 3 (Winter 1989).

Bachrach S.B. & E.J. Lawler, "The Perception of Power," *Social Forces* 55 (1976).

Baldwin, David A.   "Interdependence and Power: A Conceptual Analysis," *International Organization*, Vol. 34, No. 4 (1980) pp. 471–506.

Bergsten, C. Fred.   "From Cold War to Trade War," *International Economic Insights*, Vol. 1, No. 1 (July/August, 1990).

_____. "What to Do About the United States-Japan Economic Conflict," *Foreign Affairs*, Summer 1982.

Branson, William H. and Helen B. Junz.   "Trends in United States Trade and Comparative Advantage," *Brookings Papers in Economic Activity* No. 2 (Washington, D.C.: The Brookings Institution, 1971).

Caporaso, James A. "Dependence, Dependency, and Power in the Global System: A Structural and Behavioral Analysis," *International Organization* 32, No. 1 (Winter 1978).

Destler, I.M. and Michael Nacht.   "Beyond Mutual Recrimination: Building a Solid United States-Japan Relationship in the 1990s," *International Security*, (Winter 1990/91).

Fallows, James. "Containing Japan," *The Atlantic Monthly*, May 1989.

Gilpin, Robert. "Where Does Japan Fit In?" *Millennium: Journal of International Studies* (Winter 1989).

_____. "Three Models of the Future," *International Organization* 29 (Winter, 1975).

Helleiner, Eric. "Money and Influence: Japanese Power in the International Monetary and Financial System," *Millennium: Journal of International Studies* 18:3 (Winter 1989).

Holsti, Kal J. "Politics in Command: Foreign Trade as National Security Policy," *International Organization* 40 (Summer 1986).

Inoguchi, T. "Japan's Images and Options: Not a Challenger But a Supporter," *The Journal of Japanese Studies,* Vol. 12, No. 1, (Winter 1986).

Lake, D.A. "Beneath the Commerce of Nations: A Theory of International Economic Structures," *International Studies Quarterly* Vol. 28, 1984.

Motoo, Abe. "Foreign Aid: A Dissenter's View," *Japan Echo*, Vol. XVI, No. 1, Spring 1989.

Murphy, R. Taggart. "Power Without Purpose: The Crisis of Japan's Global Financial Dominance," *Harvard Business Review*, March-April 1989.

Nagato, Kazuhiko. "The Japan-United States Savings Rate Gap," *Economic Eye*, June 1985.

Rubinstein, Gregg. "United States-Japan Security Relations," *The Fletcher Forum*, Vol. 12, No. 1 (Winter 1988).

Russett, Bruce. "The mysterious case of vanishing hegemony: or, is Mark Twain really dead?" *International Organization*, Vol. 39, No. 2 (Spring 1985).

Sata, Seizaburo. "The United States-Japan Alliance Under Changing International Relations," *Washington Quarterly* (Summer, 1990).

_____. "The Unfolding Gulf Crisis and Japan's New Responsibility," *Japan Times Weekly*, Sept. 10-16, 1990.

Simon, S.W. "Is there a Japanese Regional Security Role?" *Journal of Northeast Asian Studies*, Vol. 5, No. 2, (Summer 1986).

Snidal, Duncan. "Limits of hegemonic stability theory," *International Organization*, Vol. 39, No. 4 (Autumn 1985).

Stogo, A.J. "If America Won't Lead," *Foreign Policy*, No. 64, Fall 1986.

Tamamoto, Masaru. "Japan's Search for a World Role," *World Policy Journal*, Vol. VII, No. 3 (Summer 1990).

Ullman, Richard H. "Redefining Security," *International Security* 8 (Summer 1983).

Vernon, Raymond. "The Japan-United States Bilateral Relationship: Its Role in the Global Economy," *The Washington Quarterly*, Vol. 13, No. 3 (Summer 1990).

Government Document and Other Sources

Challenges and Opportunities in United-States Japan Relations: A Report Submitted to the President of the United States and the Prime Minister of Japan (Washington, D.C.: United States-Japan Advisory Commission, September 1984).

Diplomacy Blue Book, 1975–1983 volumes (Tokyo: Ministry of Foreign Affairs 1975–1983).

Discriminate Deterrence A Paper by the Regional Conflict Working Group submitted to the Commission on Integrated Long-Term Strategy (Washington, D.C.: Government Printing Office, May 1988).

Economic Security in Japan (Tokyo: Ministry of International Trade and Industry (MITI), 1982).

Foreign Trade of Japan Annual volumes, 1955–1973. Japan External Trade Organization (JETRO).

Handbook of Economic Statistics, (1984). Central Intelligence Agency.

High Technology Position Paper Advisory Council on Japan-United States Economic Relations (Washington, D.C.: United States Department of Commerce, July 1985).

Indicators of Science and Technology (1984). Science and Technology Agency (Tokyo: STA, March 30, 1985).

International Cooperation Initiative (Contributing to the Peace and Prosperity of the World (Tokyo: Ministry of Foreign Affairs, January 1989).

Japan 1985: An International Comparison (Tokyo: Keizai Koho Center, 1985).

Japan's Foreign Direct Investment, 1988 Annual Report (Tokyo: Ministry of Finance, 1989).

Japan's Foreign Direct Investment by Industry and Region (Tokyo: Ministry of Finance, March 31, 1989).

Japan's Official Development Assistance 1988 Annual Report (Tokyo: Ministry of Foreign Affairs, 1989).

Japan Statistical Yearbook, 1986. Statistics Bureau, Management and Coordination Agency, Tokyo 1986.

Present Situation and Problems of Economic Cooperation (Tokyo: Ministry of International Trade and Industry, 1982).

Science and Technology Indicators (Paris: OECD, Annual Series 1980–1988).

Science, Technology and U.S. Diplomacy, 1986 Seventh annual report submitted to the Congress by the president pursuant to section 503(b) of Title V of Public Law 95–426 (Washington, D.C.: U.S. Government Printing Office, May 1986).

Statistical Handbook of Japan, 1986. (Statistics Bureau, Management and Coordination Agency, Tokyo, 1986).

The Silent Power: Japan's Identity and World Role (Tokyo: Japan Center for International Exchange, 1976).

The United States and a Unifying Europe: The Necessity of Partnership. Department of State Bulletin 69 (1801) 1973.

Transnational Corporations in World Development: Trends and Prospects (New York: United Nations Central on Transnational Corporations, 1988).

United States Industrial Outlook. United States Department of Commerce, International Trade Association, 1986 (Washington, D.C.: United States Government Printing Office, 1986).

United States Overseas Loans and Grants and Assistance from International Organizations, 1990 (Washington, D.C.: Government Printing Office, 1991).

United States Trade: Performance in 1985 and Outlook (Washington, D.C.: United States Department of Commerce, International Trade Administration, October 1986).

White Paper on Science and Technology 1985 Science and Technology Agency (Tokyo: Foreign Press Center, December 1985).

Yearbook of United States-Japan Economic Relations (Washington, D.C.: United States-Japan Trade Council, March 1979 (annual).

INDEX